"Far too many Christia⟨...⟩ too soon' when it come⟨...⟩ ⟨...⟩ ⟨...⟩ about sex. Unfortunately, this often means parents say too little, too late. Anne's book shatters this and other misconceptions parents have about teaching children about sexual topics, and in our hyper-sexualized culture, it delivers a timely and critical message."

Luke Gilkerson, author of *The Talk* and Educational Resource Manager at Covenant Eyes

"I remember seeing Anne's blog post 'Three Things You Don't Know about Your Children and Sex' go viral, and I am so excited her new book has expanded on this topic. Every parent needs to pay attention to this book."

Craig Gross, founder of iParent.tv and author of *Touchy Subjects*

"Thank you, Anne Marie Miller, for speaking out about the oft-taboo subject of kids and sex. You remind me—using loving, honest, educational words—that it won't be through sheltering or silence that we guide our kids to a place of sexual health. It will be through conversation, love, and a focus on our Creator. This book has empowered me as a mom. I recommend it."

Lisa Whittle, speaker and author of {w}hole and I Want God

"Anne Marie Miller has given a wonderful gift to parents in 5 *Things Every Parent Needs to Know about Their Kids and Sex.* Having worked with teenagers and parents for twenty-five years, I find parents are rarely prepared for having this discussion. It never seems to happen on our timeline, and the prevalence of sexual knowledge surpasses anything most parents had access to when they were children and teens. Ann Marie's book is current and on point. Read this before you think you need to, and if that time has passed, start reading now!"

Mark Matlock, president of Youth Specialties

"Honest, authentic, and essential. Anne Marie brilliantly weaves her compelling personal journey, insightful analysis, and practical suggestions into a helpful resource for every family."

John Cotton Richmond, speaker, writer, and federal human trafficking prosecutor

"This is Miller's best work. *5 Things Every Parent Needs to Know about Their Kids and Sex* is really raw and really powerful. She speaks with experience and authority and has compiled a great list of stories, interviews, tools, questions, and resources for parents to use with their kids."

Rhett Smith, MDiv, LMFT

"Anne Marie Miller has done the work. Her passion, intelligence, and talent intersect and bring us something truly important in *5 Things Every Parent Needs to Know about Their Kids and Sex*. If we are honest with ourselves, it is easy to recognize the spiritual and sexual crisis facing our children today. Miller informs and instructs with humility and compelling confidence. The intertwining of her research and her personal history gives the reader the distinct sense that she knows this topic inside and out, and it makes her determination to win back the hearts and minds of our children contagious. I am more equipped to be a better father after reading this book."

Dr. David Long, MD

5 Things

EVERY
PARENT

NEEDS TO KNOW ABOUT THEIR

Kids and Sex

ANNE MARIE MILLER

BakerBooks

a division of Baker Publishing Group
Grand Rapids, Michigan

© 2016 by Anne Marie Miller

Published by Baker Books
a division of Baker Publishing Group
P.O. Box 6287, Grand Rapids, MI 49516-6287
www.bakerbooks.com

Printed in the United States of America

Library of Congress Cataloging-in-Publication Data
Names: Miller, Anne Marie, 1980– author.
Title: 5 things every parent needs to know about their kids and sex / Anne Marie Miller.
Other titles: Five things every parent needs to know about their kids and sex
Description: Grand Rapids, MI : Baker Books, 2016. | Includes bibliographical references.
Identifiers: LCCN 2015040653 | ISBN 9780801018992 (pbk.)
Subjects: LCSH: Parenting—Religious aspects—Christianity. | Child rearing—Religious aspects—Christianity. | Sex—Religious aspects--Christianity. | Sex instruction.
Classification: LCC BV4529 .M545 2016 | DDC 241/.664—dc23
LC record available at http://lccn.loc.gov/2015040653

Unless otherwise indicated, Scripture quotations are from the New King James Version. Copyright © 1982 by Thomas Nelson, Inc. Used by permission. All rights reserved.

Scripture quotations labeled NASB are from the New American Standard Bible®, copyright © 1960, 1962, 1963, 1968, 1971, 1972, 1973, 1975, 1977, 1995 by The Lockman Foundation. Used by permission.

Scripture quotations labeled NIV are from the Holy Bible, New International Version®. NIV®. Copyright © 1973, 1978, 1984, 2011 by Biblica, Inc.™ Used by permission of Zondervan. All rights reserved worldwide. www.zondervan.com

Scripture quotations labeled NLT are from the Holy Bible, New Living Translation, copyright © 1996, 2004, 2007 by Tyndale House Foundation. Used by permission of Tyndale, Carol Stream, Illinois 60188. All rights reserved.

In circumstances in which permission could not be obtained, the names and insignificant details of the stories in this book have been modified in order to protect the identities of the people mentioned. Some anecdotes and characters may also be composites of multiple illustrations and people. If the situation warranted reporting, rest assured those responsible took all appropriate legal measures and action. Any other resemblance of any person or any situation, real or fictional, is entirely coincidental.

This publication is intended to provide helpful and informative material on the subjects addressed. Readers should consult their personal health professionals before adopting any of the suggestions in this book or drawing inferences from it. The author and publisher expressly disclaim responsibility for any adverse effects arising from the use or application of the information contained in this book.

Author is represented by the literary agency of Alive Communications, Inc., 7680 Goddard Street, Suite 200, Colorado Springs, CO 80920, www.alivecommunications.com.

16 17 18 19 20 21 22   7 6 5 4 3 2 1

In keeping with biblical principles of creation stewardship, Baker Publishing Group advocates the responsible use of our natural resources. As a member of the Green Press Initiative, our company uses recycled paper when possible. The text paper of this book is composed in part of post-consumer waste.

Contents

5

One Thing You Need to Know before Reading This Book

This is a book about sex.

Things may get a little awkward.

And that's the thing we're going to change.

Sex is not awkward (well, it can be . . . *in a fun way* . . . more on that later).

Sex is beautiful.

Sex isn't just a physical act—it's a spiritual one.

It's emotional.

It's relational.

Our sexuality isn't something that should be hiding in dark corners; it should be discussed honestly, joyously, openly.

And while sex is a brilliant part of our lives, it's also an intimate part of our lives.

That doesn't mean we need to keep quiet about it.

Since the day the first humans knew they were naked—and they were ashamed—we have been trying to put as many proverbial fig leaves as possible between our sexuality and one another.

It's time to start peeling off the layers one by one.

Yes, this is a book about sex, and we explore sensitive topics like pornography, abuse, and trafficking. You might find some of the things you read disturbing or offensive. Sometimes the things you read *are* disturbing or offensive.

But sexuality is not.

I've worked very closely with my publisher, my editors, and various contributors to communicate the truth and context of the often-scary reality in which we live without being gratuitous. It is not my goal to shock you with unnecessary details, yet at the same time the subject matter at hand has often been distorted from a beautiful part of being divinely human to the unimaginable and the unpleasant. I have attempted to walk this fine line with decency and wisdom and hope you will walk along that line with me with grace and understanding.

Author's Note

Throughout history, people have approached the topic of sexuality from many vantage points—some from a place of silence and shame, and others from a place *where anything goes, whatever feels good must be good*—without thought or consequence.

In regard to sex, people from religious circles often hold the point of view that leans more in favor of silence and shame. We don't talk about sex. Sex is seen as dirty. A hush-hush attitude can be the impetus behind shame complexes in children (and adults). It can also prohibit natural sexual exploration or experimentation.

Growing up in a conservative, Southern, *and* religious culture, sex was not discussed in my home, my school, or my church. Except for our youth group's annual True Love Waits event, talking about sex was off-limits. And at the conference, all we were told was "Don't have sex."

Nobody dared ask *why*.

Keeping talk about sex under wraps definitely had an impact on my formative years (I'll share my story in a few pages). And now, after twenty-something years, with God's providence and maybe a little bit of his humor, he has firmly planted in my heart a passion to change the conversation.

Sex is not a subject to avoid. Sex is a gift from God to us to celebrate and enjoy.

We, the church, cannot keep quiet about the subject of sex any longer. Because of the broken world in which we live, adults and children are presented with a distorted image of sexuality at each and every turn. This distorted image affects us in all areas of our lives, including our spirituality, our relationships, and our worldview.

As you work through this book, you'll inevitably see that my conservative religious background didn't scar me for life. I'm still involved in church, I work in full-time ministry, and, to set the tone of this book, I love sex!* My beliefs (having been shaped by what I understand the Bible to say and my own life experiences) construct and direct my views on sex. This does not mean I have everything figured out, nor am I suggesting that I am correct in every situation. However, my faith in God and belief in the truth of the Scriptures will be apparent as you read.

My hope in writing this book is simply to educate, encourage, and equip parents who share similar Christian beliefs by providing statistics, stories, and resources that will help them engage in gracious and life-giving conversations about sex.

With that said, please know that I am not here to convert others with differing viewpoints. I hope those who believe differently, either inside or outside the Christian faith, will

*Oversharing? Maybe. But it's a book on sex. You should probably get used to this.

read one perspective by one woman and use it as a jumping point for conversation . . . even if we disagree.

Some people may think what I research or suggest is too conservative or religious or prohibitive. Others may think it's too open and broad or that my experience and advice are not conservative enough. *I fully realize this and ask for your grace in those areas where our thoughts differ.*

This is not a book full of doom and gloom. It is not a book telling you *how* as much as it is sharing *why* this conversation is important. It's not a book about rules; it's about redeeming a much-needed conversation.

I'm not here to frighten you or encourage you to move off the grid, far away from the dangers of technology and modern Western culture (though sometimes it's tempting, isn't it?). I simply want to inform you of the things I've learned from my years of talking to kids just like yours in communities just like yours. I'm here to offer you the tools and knowledge that will best aid you in initiating and continuing the conversation about sex in your home—with as little anxiety and awkwardness as possible.

This Book Is a Starting Point

You can read this book from cover to cover or just peek at the things you feel are most relevant to you and your family at the moment. Use it as a reference guide.

During the course of writing this book, I told my publisher each chapter could stand alone as its own book. Sex is a beautiful and complex topic, as are the physical, social, and psychological effects it has on us. If you want to learn more about one of the five things I've addressed, visit

5ThingsBook.com, email me, or ask a pastor, a doctor, or a counselor. Much more information is available as you navigate these topics with your children.

Before you dip your toes in the water, here's a quick overview of what's ahead:

In the preface, you'll learn a little bit about me and why my personal history is relevant to this book. In the introduction, we'll run through a basic understanding of the theology of sex. It's important to begin this conversation with why sex is important to God. We'll look at the purpose of sex from a scriptural perspective and explore why God cares about it. We'll also talk briefly about how we, as adults, view sex, and how your own personal history is significant to this conversation as well.

In chapter 1, we'll look at the sexual development of children and when and how to initiate conversations about sex. We'll discuss the degree of detail and content appropriate for particular ages and why these conversations are necessary, even imperative, in the first place.

In chapter 2, we'll debunk the myth that your child is the exception to the rule. The fact is that parents can take every precaution available, but at some point in time, children will need to learn how to handle their sexuality and encounters with sex on their own.

In chapter 3, we'll explore what largely informs society's view of sex: mainstream media. We'll examine how we digest the media we consume and how it affects our beliefs and behavior. We'll also delve into four media staples: television, video games, movies, and music.

Of course, our media consumption doesn't end there. In chapter 4, we'll look at how the internet and new technology is changing the way kids are educating themselves about sex. We'll also explore pornography's impact on our individual health, as well as on public health, and examine the correlation between the sex industry and sex trafficking and why it's important to offer our children the big-picture repercussions of pornography.

Finally, chapter 5 addresses some tender issues, particularly identifying and healing from sexual abuse. We'll discuss the signs of sexual abuse, explore the reasons why survivors of sexual abuse rarely speak up, and determine how we should talk to our children about such a sensitive topic.

If you're starting to feel a little overwhelmed, it's okay. I'm right there with you, which is why we'll conclude the book with the most important message of all: *there is hope*. There is hope for you, for your children, and for your family. There's even hope for the world. In the Resources for the Conversation section and on 5ThingsBook.com, you'll find practical books, websites, and other materials that will help equip you to talk to your kids about sex.

I have never been more certain about anything in my life than I am about this: it is time to be brave about communicating openly and frequently about healthy biblical sexuality. Chances are that as you read through this book and begin to talk with your children about sex, you will see, if you haven't already, how the culture of sex in our world is changing at lightning speed.

Since 2012, anytime I've given a talk about sex and almost every time I've sat down to write or edit this book, the enemy (we'll call him Satan or the devil or whatever word best describes him to you) has attacked. I know that sounds a little crazy.

Time and time again, just days before I was to share my
story and resources at an event, I would end up in the emergency room with a different health scare. I got a concussion
and experienced the sudden onset of the flu, pneumonia,
and bronchitis (at the same time)—all issues affecting my
ability to speak. During the course of writing this book or
other material on this topic, something would inevitably
interrupt me, whether it was a common cold (but just bad
enough to make my brain too fuzzy to write coherently), a
major issue with our home, an ill family member, a friend
newly diagnosed with cancer, the death of a loved one, or
even, most recently, a shooting in the store next to the café
where I was writing. I was thirty minutes into writing about
how parents can't always protect their children when a police
officer entered the café and instructed everyone to evacuate
immediately. As I left, a SWAT team stood shoulder to shoulder, their automatic rifles drawn, waiting for a gunman in
the store next door. Somebody had been shot less than one
hundred feet from me, and while everyone in the café was
safe, I was tempted to play the worst-case scenario over and
over again in my mind. *What if the shooter had chosen the
café instead of the store next door?**

Later, during the editing process of this book, I became
pregnant. But then I miscarried, which required an emergency
surgery and more time off. And then my laptop suddenly
went missing for two weeks—and I had not saved my most
recent edits.

Satan wants me to be afraid. He wants to prevent me
from talking about this topic. And he wants you to be afraid

---

*They caught the shooter, for what it's worth, and nobody was seriously
harmed in the incident.

too. I don't blame every horrible thing that happens in life on the enemy, but there are some things I can't dismiss as coincidence.

We are in a fight. We frequently point to the media, pornography, and sex as the enemy, but these things, especially sex, are *not* the true enemy. God has given us sex as a beautiful way to express love to our spouse. The media and pornography are tools the enemy uses to break us down, enslave us, and cause us to feel shame instead of strength and hopelessness instead of hope.

Our enemy is Satan.

We are all, each one of us, in the heat of the battle. I know because I am feeling the heat. I'm just one person out of many who is sharing this message of freedom and hope, and I know others are fighting to speak up too.

Here are some things you can do to strengthen your fight:

1. **Pray.** Pray always. Pray for your family, your church leaders, and the people who are called and committed to sharing the message of God's grace and hope to those broken by addictive behaviors and to those negatively impacted by damaging images and messages about sex.

2. **Create family values.** Create and adopt a set of family values to guide you as you work through these chapters and as you engage in difficult conversations with your children. I've put together a list here, but feel free to create your own guidelines as well. The family values listed below will also be included in other chapters for your reference. It's important to note that while this book is primarily about sex, our lives are about so much

more. These values are applicable to all areas of our lives. If good values are established together as a family, each member will have a sense of ownership and responsibility and want to fulfill them.

Family Values

- We believe God created sex to be a worshipful experience between husband and wife* that brings glory to him.
- We believe that because we live in a fallen world and will constantly face distorted views of sexuality, we must learn to identify and process these views in a healthy and biblically sound manner.
- We believe in honest conversation, even if it feels uncomfortable, antiquated, or old-fashioned.
- We believe everybody is created in God's image, and no one should be abused or exploited for any reason.
- We believe we should not be ashamed of sex or sexuality— ever.
- We believe in showing grace, mercy, and love in every circumstance, even toward people whose beliefs we don't agree with or understand.
- We believe in the healing and redemptive power of the love of God, who sacrificed his Son, Jesus Christ, for our sins.
- We believe in having integrity in our thoughts, words, and actions by demonstrating God's love to everyone, including ourselves, regardless of past or present circumstances.
- We believe in asking for help when we need it.
- We believe in relying on the power of God and prayer, as well as being accountable to our family and friends when we struggle.

3. **Find Freedom.** Statistics indicate that more than half the people reading this book are waging a battle of their

---

*I understand homosexuality is a very widely debated topic in the Christian culture. If you're tempted to mentally check out and not finish this book because of my belief, I encourage you to hang in there. I go into a little more detail about this later.

Author's Note

own. If this is you, please get help. Tell someone. Tell just one person. Do whatever is necessary, even if it's extreme, to seek freedom. We will talk about this more in the introduction.

> We believe God created sex to be a worshipful experience between husband and wife that brings glory to him.

4. **Love your enemies.** We shouldn't get angry with the media or the pornography industry. We need to pray for the people trapped in the sex industry. A lot of them don't want to be there. Pray that God's love is so bright it will overpower the darkness they live in.

5. **Talk to your church leaders.** Conversations about sexuality, pornography, and abuse should not be limited to our families. The church is not exempt from this conversation. Speak with the person who directs your church's adult and young adult ministries about the necessity of having this kind of conversation within your church. Consider leading a prayer ministry specifically geared toward those who are trapped in a cycle of sexual abuse or sin. Engage your church in a prayerful revival. Rely on God to deliver those who are trapped and use others who aren't to help them heal.

Talking about sex, pornography, abuse, and trafficking is not an easy task. Let's acknowledge this fact early on and know that these growing pains are necessary and good. These conversations, though difficult, will positively impact your family—and quite possibly families around the world. With God's help, we've got this. We can reshape our culture with humility, surrender, and proactive communication with our children and other parents.

Let's redeem the conversation.

Peace in the name of Christ,
Anne Marie Miller[1]

Contributors

I convey my most sincere gratitude to these well-respected experts who graciously offered their words of wisdom and counsel to bring more specific education, research, and stories to this book.

I thank Dr. Russell Moore, president of the Ethics & Religious Liberty Commission of the Southern Baptist Convention; Rhett Smith, MDiv, MSFMT; Jen Sandbulte; Olivia Pelts, MA, LPC; Dr. David R. Long, MD; Laura A. W. Pratt, attorney-at-law; Corporal Jimmy Fair, Lubbock Police Department; Linda Smith, former congresswoman and founder of Shared Hope International.

Medical and psychological editorial reviews were generously contributed by David R. Long, MD, and Rhett Smith, MDiv, MSFMT.

I offer a very special thank-you to Crystal Renaud, CLPC, for her diligent assistance in helping compile these resources. Crystal is the founder and executive director of WHOLE Women Ministries whose projects include Dirty Girls Ministries and

WHOLE Women Weekend. Crystal holds a BS in psychology from Liberty University and four certifications, including one in professional life coaching. In her book *Dirty Girls Come Clean*, she shares her story of freedom from pornography use, which she hopes will bring other women out of oppression as well. Her work has been featured by the *New York Times*, *ABC News*, CNN, *Christianity Today*, *700 Club*, and more.

Preface

My Story

Please allow me to introduce myself before we go much further. My name is Anne Marie Miller, which I'm guessing you saw on the cover. I'm in my midthirties and have been married to my husband, Tim, a youth pastor, since 2013. I grew up in the church—the daughter of a Southern Baptist minister—with a passion for learning the Bible. I was the honors student, the athlete, the girl who got along with everyone—from the weird kids to the popular crowd. It was a good life. I was raised in a good home.

In 1996, I was sixteen, and the internet was new. After my family moved from a sheltered, conservative life in west Texas (think *Friday Night Lights*) to the diverse culture of Dallas, I found myself lonely, curious, and confused.

Because of my volatile life circumstances at the time—I was struggling with my new environment and dealing with the stress of my dad's depression—I reached out to a local youth pastor. I needed help and went to what was familiar. I asked him for assistance in launching a Bible study, and he offered some materials for leading a prayer rally at my high school. A few weeks later our relationship changed, and for the next six months—most of my junior year of high school—he sexually abused me.

Sex was one of those things my family and my church kept in the dark. There was no talk about "the birds and the bees" for me. The combination of teenage hormones, the variety of new words I heard at school and on the radio, and the sexual nature of my abuse left me feeling lost and confused. I couldn't ask my parents about it. I thought they'd ground me for life. Plus, pastors were (wrongly) godlike in my view, so I felt like I couldn't tell anyone about what that youth pastor was doing to me. I didn't want to get him in trouble even though I knew what was happening to me was illegal. I felt like I must have done something to "deserve" the abuse. And I couldn't talk to my friends. Most of them were sexually active, and I was embarrassed about my lack of knowledge and experience. I didn't know what certain words meant and was too afraid to ask.

Instead, I turned to the internet for education, and what began as an innocent pursuit of knowledge quickly escalated into a coping mechanism. Soon that coping mechanism—looking at online pornography—became a compulsive behavior.[1] When I looked at pornography, I experienced feelings of love and safety—at least for a brief moment. But after those brief moments of relief disappeared, I felt ashamed and confused. Pornography provided me both an emotional and a sexual escape. It was medication.

I carried this secret and the heavy shame that accompanied it for years. I knew guys looked at porn—that was culturally common and even somewhat socially acceptable. But a girl? A preacher's kid? Surely there was something wrong with me, something dark and perverted. Why else would the youth pastor take advantage of me? Why else would I seek out the images and videos I did? Why else would they make me feel better?

My Rock-Bottom Moment

As soon as I graduated high school, I found a successful job at one of the first dot-com companies. I took home a great paycheck, enjoyed all the luxuries it afforded, and was close to my friends and family. The year before, shortly after my nineteenth birthday, my longtime boyfriend had proposed to me, and I had said yes. I was engaged. But despite all that, my online habits were affecting my off-line life.

I'd reconnected with a male friend from high school through the internet. We chatted online at night and eventually met in person again. It had been two years since I'd seen him. I promised myself it was an innocent friendship and denied how my heart raced when I was with him. We began to see each other more and more—until one day, we were caught.

My fiancé knew I had a time-consuming job and was gracious about it. He worked at a law firm, and we had planned for me to cut back on my hours once we were married. He and I were supposed to go on a date one night, but I called him from work to cancel, telling him my colleagues were going out after work and I needed to be there. He understood. What I didn't say was that "people from work" meant my old high school friend, a lie I justified by having him meet me at my office, so *technically*, he was a person from work. I assuaged my guilt in technicalities.

We went to see a movie. When my fiancé called my old Nokia cell phone during the movie, I thought I'd pressed the end button but unknowingly hit the talk button instead. He overheard the movie and the bits of conversation my "friend" and I were having.

Later that night, my fiancé confronted me. I confessed— yes, I'd been spending time with another man. Yes, we had a romantic relationship. When my fiancé asked if I loved this other man, I didn't know how to answer. All I knew was that I felt *really* good around him. So I said yes. Yes, I loved him.

My fiancé and I sat in my living room. I gave him back our engagement ring. We cried. He kept asking, "Why? Why? Why?" And I kept saying, "I don't know. I don't know. I don't know." He left in tears. I never saw him again.*

That night, I stared at myself in the mirror. In some ways, it was like staring at a stranger. I remember touching my cheeks, wondering if the person in the reflection was me. All I knew was that something was wrong with my mind.

I knew lying was wrong. I knew cheating was wrong. I knew my selfishness was wrong. I knew the way I was living my life was wrong. I wondered where the good preacher's kid went. I looked in the mirror and said out loud, "You weren't raised to be a porn-watching, materialistic, two-timing slut."

---

*Based on his present circumstances, there is a relatively good chance my ex-fiancé will read this book. If you do read this, please know how sorry I am for the way I mistreated you. I'm so glad you have found happiness with your wife and family.

The word *slut* slithered out of my mouth like a hiss. I was disgusted with myself for saying it, but at the same time, I also had an epiphany. *Wait. The "real me" never would have said the word* slut. *Why did I say it?*

I closed my eyes. I saw the word *slut* painted in a million different colors and fonts. It was like I was looking at a computer screen through the lens of my mind's eye.

In that moment I realized the connection: my porn habit was somehow part of the demise of my relationship. Pornography—the words, the messages, and even the actions—had infiltrated my mind and my life.

That was the night I walked over to my computer, a purple and beige Compaq Presario, unplugged the tower, marched it down the concrete stairs of my apartment building and across the parking lot, and placed it next to an overflowing dumpster. That was the night, disgusted and frustrated by my lack of control and online pornography bingeing, I threw away my computer. I'd hit rock bottom.

Two years later, at the age of twenty-one, I finally opened up to a friend, *only* because she confessed her struggle with pornography use to me first. We began a path toward healing and for the last fifteen years, though it's not been a perfect journey, I can say with great confidence that God has set me free from the desire to look at pornography and from the shame I carried for so long.

Speaking Up about Freedom

Over the last decade, I've had the opportunity to share my story in a variety of venues with hundreds of thousands of teens, college students, men, and women. Sharing my story is always a little awkward, but it's a gift I've embraced over time.* It honestly doesn't even feel like it's my story anymore.

Instead, it's a story God has redeemed for good. I am no longer the woman at the well, ashamed of her past. Instead, I am the woman at the well *after* Jesus meets her—the woman who, despite the shame and embarrassment and awkwardness and fear, can't wait to tell others what he did for me.

After Jesus met this Samaritan woman, she couldn't contain her joy.

> The woman left her water jar beside the well and ran back to the village, telling everyone, "Come and see a man who told me everything I ever did! Could he possibly be the Messiah?" So the people came streaming from the village to see him.
>
> John 4:28–30 NLT

Like the Samaritan woman at the well, I can't wait to share that there's hope and freedom down the road. And beyond that, there's joy!

I was twenty-seven years old when I left my full-time job at a church to become a full-time author and speaker. I worried people wouldn't listen to me because I was so young. Many of the audiences I spoke to were comprised of parents and people in their midforties. Although I always felt a little timid speaking to these listeners, I drew strength from the truth that I was called by God to share my story of redemption with them. Over time I came to understand that many men and women, no matter their age, related to my experiences. We shared a common history: sexual abuse, struggles with pornography, codependency, feelings of worthlessness, and

---

*I call it the spiritual gift of awkwardness.

issues with body image. Although hearing people's stories was painful, seeing God heal and transform others—and continue to heal me—was rewarding.

In my early thirties, I returned to school to study the science behind addiction and the sociology behind family dynamics. My goal was to bring a technical understanding of sexuality into the realm of religion and faith, where I saw it was deeply lacking. During this time, more student ministries and universities began to ask me to speak. Now my fear was that I was too old. What twelve-year-old boy wants to hear someone his mom's age talk about sex? *Awkward!* Yet I sensed a calling to share with students how God has freed me from the shame and actions of my past. I yearned to assure them that they aren't alone (because everyone always truly thinks they are alone). One college dean referred to me as "the grenade we're tossing into our student body to get the conversation of sex started." He and other administrators had realized that sweeping these topics under the rug caused their students to feel trapped, obsessed, and ashamed. I will continue to share my testimony in this capacity as long as there is a student in front of me who needs to hear it. When I finish speaking at these events, I'm always surprised to see how many students line up to talk with me afterward. They want and need to share their stories, their desire to be free from their struggles with pornography, their battles with shame, and their pain from abuse—struggles, battles, and pain no one knew about.[2]

An Unexpected Shift

The core of my ministry completely changed in the summer of 2013 when I entered a world few souls in my profession dare to venture into: junior high church summer camps. From Canada to Illinois, my husband Tim and I spent weeks with junior high students, equal parts terrified of their emerging hormones and enamored with their not-quite-teenagers-yet innocence.

The last night of the last camp was pivotal for me. In fact, it prompted the idea for this book.

The camp directors (who were youth pastors at the church sponsoring the camp) asked me to share my story with the junior high girls, most of whom were ten to thirteen years old. I had shared a little each day, but the last night culminated in hours of open one-on-one confession and counseling in the back of the auditorium. As the girls tearfully shared their stories with me, I was forced to mask my shock and horror regarding what they confessed. At the same time, I noticed three things in common with almost all the stories and confessions I heard that night:

- They learned about sex from Google (usually around the age of eight or nine years old) and had seen pornography.
- If they'd been sexually abused, molested, or violated in any way, they didn't tell anyone about it (until me).
- They believed they would get in trouble if they told their parents either of the above statements because their parents were good Christian parents and their families went to church.

When I mentioned what I'd learned to the youth pastor at the night's end, I'll never forget what he said: "The thing is that most parents think their kid is the exception."

At the end of the evening, I collapsed onto the bed in our camp room. Tim comforted me as I wrestled with what to do with all the information I'd heard over the summer. The next day I penned a blog post titled "Three Things Parents Don't Know about Their Kids and Sex." Within seventy-two hours, the post went viral, with more than 1.5 million people reading and sharing it across social media channels. What I'd learned at church camp clearly connected with many parents who wanted to protect their children but didn't know where to begin.

Now more than ever I am aware of just *how little* parents know about what's happening with their children and sex. Please don't hear this as an insult to you, your heart, your intention, or your love for your kids. *It's not.* And because I haven't experienced years of parenting (yet), I feel terribly inadequate telling you this.

But I can't *not* tell you. A mentor and close friend recently reminded me that the two people who talked about marriage the most in the Bible were Jesus and Paul, neither of whom was married. God's call is God's call, and I am confident in my call to speak out on this topic. Those closest to me affirm this.

After seeing the innocence in the eyes of ten-year-old girls who've carried secrets *nobody*, let alone children, should carry, and after hearing some of the most horrific accounts from students I've heard in recent years, I cannot go one more day without pleading with you to talk with your children.

Would you prefer your son learn what a fetish is from you or from searching Google Images? How would you feel if your daughter came home from a slumber party singing the lyrics to an inappropriate song? That happened to a friend of mine. She overheard her eight-year-old daughter singing the lyrics to "All about That Bass," a song that refers to a young woman's curvy hips as something guys like "to hold at night." When my friend asked her daughter where she heard it, her daughter replied, "We watched the video on Taylor's iPad." Of course, in conducting proper research for this book, I also watched the video, which includes a model wrapped in plastic wrap, sexy poses and dancing, along with a couple of ten-year-old girls dancing to the song in the video. Another friend of mine learned her daughter first saw porn in the church bathroom via an image on a fifth-grader's phone.

Do the right thing, the hard thing, and talk to your children about sex for their sake and the sake of your family. If we don't have these conversations now, I am terrified the enemy will continue to steal hope and joy from our youngest generation, paralyzing their ability to advance the kingdom of God as they mature. We can't let this happen anymore. It's going to be hard, but you don't have to do it alone. This book (along with your church, your community, your doctors, your counselors, and your friends) can guide you through the process.

Introduction

Sex Is a Gift from God

Sex doesn't make sense unless we understand that it is holy.

—Dr. Tim Alan Gardner

A few years ago, a conservative university asked me to share my story at their weekly chapel and invite students to open up confidentially to counselors and student leaders if they had been abused or were wrestling with any questions about sex. About ten minutes into my talk, I could tell by the looks of sheer terror on their faces that it was very likely the students, especially the girls, had never heard such a candid (yet still very appropriate) message about sex. At the end of my time, I said a prayer and with every good intention, uttered the words, "God, I thank you for the gift of sex you gave to us," finished praying, and walked off the stage. The dean of spiritual life followed up my speech with instructions on how those who felt they needed to talk with someone could find counselors or student leaders to help.

I had some time before my flight back home, so as I relaxed on a bench in the warm sun, I pulled up Twitter* on my phone and saw that a few students from the college had followed me. A social media rabbit trail ensued, leading me to a tweet I resisted responding to.

One of the students said, "Did our chapel speaker just thank GOD for SEX?! I thought this was a Christian college!"

At first, I laughed to myself and composed a reply that said, "Who was I supposed to thank? Buddha?"

Before I let my sarcasm get the best of me, I quickly deleted my reply and let it go. As it turned out, that individual wasn't alone in his dismay. Many students tweeted about how they attended that college because they wanted to learn more about God, not about sex.

As I mentioned previously, separating God and sex into categories of "good" and "bad" isn't uncommon in religious circles. Sex is an uncomfortable subject for most people, especially students. Inevitably, a string of questions follow, including "How far is too far? Is kissing a sin? Holding hands? What about masturbation?" The truth is that Scripture doesn't specifically answer every question related to sex, but before we can dig into the specifics of how a biblical view of sexuality is defined, we must first address the foundational question: What does God think about sex?

Theologians have studied sex and theology for thousands of years. Catalogs of books have been written that delve into the original Hebrew and Greek texts of the Scriptures. Some of what the Bible says about sex is completely clear to us,

*Back when Twitter was cool.

especially when we look at the original language and historical contexts. Other topics aren't addressed specifically. And some subjects—like masturbation—aren't mentioned at all.*

To set our expectations appropriately, let me remind you that this is *only one* small section of one book. In a limited space, I'm going to do my best to present you with a basic theology of sex. This chapter is meant to offer a framework to guide you when questions arise. Understanding why God cares about sex (and its many facets) is essential to each and every conversation you'll have with your children about it. But please know this chapter is simply the tip of the iceberg, so to speak. In the Resources for the Conversation section, I recommend a few books I used for my research in case the subject interests you more.

What's the Purpose of Sex?

We know sex is a gift from God because Scripture tells us exactly that.[1] According to author Denny Burk in his book *What is the Meaning of Sex?*, God intends his gift of sex to fulfill two purposes—the *subordinate purpose* and the *ultimate purpose*.

Let me give you an example to help distinguish between the two purposes. Think about a dining room table. You could find a hundred purposes for a dining room table, but the ultimate purpose, of course, is to offer family and friends a place to eat meals (and in my family's case, the place under which our dogs can eat the food we drop).

One of my favorite things to do is to decorate our dining room table with fresh flowers. So my dining room table *also*

---

*I'm personally mystified as to why masturbation isn't mentioned in the Bible. It's on my list of questions to ask God once I enter those pearly gates.

serves as an expression of my love for flowers and my desire to decorate. I'm not sure about your dining room table, but mine also collects mail and keys (and dust—who am I kidding?). Most days, I also write books (like this one!) at my dining room table. All the latter purposes I mentioned are subordinate purposes of a dining room table.

Let's explore another example. I have a wristwatch I frequently wear. If you're a woman, you know how difficult it can be to find one watch to match all your jewelry. This one fits the bill because it's made of silver, gold, and bronze, so regardless of what I'm wearing on a particular day, it always matches. Even though its subordinate purpose is as an accessory, my watch's ultimate purpose is to tell time.

So how do a dining room table and a watch relate to the purpose of sex? Much like my table and watch both encompass subordinate and ultimate purposes, many theologians and students of biblical sexuality link the purposes of sex to subordinate and ultimate purposes.

The three **subordinate** purposes of sex are to (1) reproduce, (2) consummate marriage, and (3) experience pleasure.

The one **ultimate** purpose of sex is to bring glory to God.

Let's take a look at what the Bible says.

Subordinate Purpose #1: Reproduction

Let the earth bring forth the living creature according to its kind.

Genesis 1:24

Before man and woman were created, God gave every living thing—the creatures of the air, sea, and land—the command to fill the earth with their own kind.[2] From the very beginning of life, God intended sex for reproduction. Reproduction wasn't God's only purpose for sex, but it was definitely one purpose. Adam and Eve were also given the responsibility to populate the earth with their kind—humans created in the image of God. That's a pretty big task to accomplish, so I imagine they jumped at the opportunity every chance they got.*

God could have used any boring, mundane way for Adam and Eve to bring children into the world. He could have made reproduction happen via a secret handshake or maybe a special dance where the bodies of a man and a woman didn't even touch. He even could have created us without sexual organs. God could have made reproduction simply an automatic function of our bodies. But he didn't—because he had a greater plan in mind when he created sex, a way for him to accomplish *all* his purposes. Procreation was one of God's first subordinate purposes for sex. It was the first purpose mentioned in Scripture, but I don't believe that gives it any more or less weight than the other two subordinate purposes (consummation and pleasure). As we continue learning about the purposes of sex, it's easy to see how they all tie together.

Subordinate Purpose #2: Consummation

> For this reason a man shall leave his father and his mother, and be joined to his wife; and they shall become one flesh.
>
> Genesis 2:24 NASB

We don't know how much time passed between the creation of Adam and Eve[3] and the fall in Genesis 3, but we can

---

*(Insert winky face here.)

be pretty confident, since God ordained them to "be fruitful and multiply" (Gen. 1:28 NASB), that they had a sexual relationship before sin entered into the world. The second purpose for sex was for man to be joined to his wife, and "they shall become one flesh."

As we will see later, the apostle Paul quoted Genesis 2:24 in his letters to both the Ephesians and the Corinthians. It sets the precedent for the design of a marital relationship: becoming "one flesh" allows a man and his wife to complete their marriage.

Subordinate Purpose #3: Pleasure

> If I should find you outside,
> I would kiss you;
> I would not be despised.
> I would lead you and bring you
> into the house.
> Song of Solomon 8:1–2*

Ah, sex and pleasure. I'm going to elaborate on this purpose for a few extra pages because, let's be honest, a lot of us have questions about the connection between sex and pleasure. Sure, we may know God designed it that way. But because of myriad external circumstances, many of us find it difficult to equate sex with pleasure.

I can relate. Because of the sexual abuse I experienced as a teen, it was difficult for me to even *think* about sex as something enjoyable until I went through a healing process.

*Abbreviated for space. But seriously, go read the whole book of Song of Solomon, preferably out loud to your spouse, with candles lit and some chocolate and wine (or grape juice, depending on your denomination) available.

I learned to forgive. I went to counseling specifically focused on lessening and removing the traumatic effects of sexual abuse.[4] I grieved what happened—deeply. I sought advice from friends. It took time, and I'm still in counseling and always seeking support, but I can honestly say the abuse in my past does not affect my ability to enjoy sex with my husband in the present.

Even if you don't have a history of abuse, many people who grew up in the church have received inaccurate messages about sex. My sweet friend and across-the-street neighbor Amy wrote about this recently.

> It's amazing, the mentality I had about our wedding day. For twenty-three years I was told, "No, no, no." Then with a few words spoken by a preacher, magically it was "Yes!" and all would be perfect.
>
> Fast forward through five years of arguments, tears, blaming, and frustration over sex. You see, there were a few lies I had come to believe about sex. Lies maybe not explicitly stated but communicated nonetheless.

One of these lies was that sex would be instantly awesome. Amy writes,

> If we would just wait, then we would somehow be automatic sexperts like in romance novels or movies. Even youth pastors would say how amazing sex is when you're married.
>
> But the truth is, more often than not, at first sex is awkward and clumsy. Sexual chemistry can take time to develop. It would have been nice to know these things in advance so our expectations might have been more realistic.
>
> Furthermore, the truth is, sometimes we just don't feel like having sex. Sex can sometimes be painful. Yes, it can be

amazing but—just like everything else in life worth learning—
you have to practice to get better. At least the practice can be
fun.[5]

Before Adam and Eve sinned against God, the world was
pure and unadulterated. Everything was in perfect harmony,
shalom, where nothing was missing and nothing was broken. Because God is good, and because the Bible says what
he creates is good, we know God created sex to be good.
He created our nerve endings to spark and our erogenous
zones to be stimulated. He wired our brain to release intense
chemicals when our spouse whispers a certain word in our
ear or touches us in a particular way.

I don't doubt that Adam and Eve fully experienced this pleasure the way God originally intended it. Unencumbered by the
baggage of fear and shame, their relationship must have been
overwhelming in the best way possible. They were able to give
themselves to each other fully and completely—without anxiety, body image hang-ups, or shame. "They were both naked,
the man and his wife, and were not ashamed" (Gen. 2:25).

When Adam and Eve sinned against God by eating from
the Tree of Knowledge, a cosmic moment occurred that forever altered history. Fear and shame instantly entered the
world, and "the eyes of both of them were opened, and they
knew they were naked; and they sewed fig leaves together
and made themselves coverings. And they heard the sound of
the LORD God walking in the garden in the cool of the day,
and Adam and his wife hid themselves from the presence of
the LORD God among the trees in the garden" (Gen. 3:7–8).

Some translations interpret the phrase "the eyes of both of
them were opened" to mean that Adam and Eve gained immediate knowledge. The minute they sinned, Adam and Eve

were immediately separated from God's perfect design for sex, and from that moment on, people have tried to reconcile God's intended ideas for sex with a sexually broken world.

This brokenness, however, does not have to diminish the pleasure of sex, as God designed it, within marriage. Even after the fall, Scripture offers us many examples of the joy of sex in marriage:

> You have ravished my heart
> My sister, my spouse;
> You have ravished my heart
> With one look of your eyes,
> With one link of your necklace.
> How fair is your love,
> My sister, my spouse!
> How much better than wine is your love,
> And the scent of your perfumes
> Than all spices!
>
> Song of Solomon 4:9–10

> The wine goes down smoothly for my beloved,
> Moving gently the lips of sleepers.
> I am my beloved's,
> And his desire is toward me.
>
> Come, my beloved,
> Let us go forth to the field;
> Let us lodge in the villages.
> Let us get up early to the vineyards;
> Let us see if the vine has budded,
> Whether the grape blossoms are open,
> And the pomegranates are in bloom.
> There I will give you my love.
>
> Song of Solomon 7:9–12

Let your fountain be blessed
    And rejoice with the wife of your youth
As a loving deer and a graceful doe,
    Let her breasts satisfy you at all times;
And always be enraptured with her love.

Proverbs 5:18–19

(Phew. Please allow me a moment to collect myself.)

My husband laughed when he read the above parenthetical statement. "Are they going to let you keep that in the book?" I shrugged and said, "Why not?" The Bible isn't erotica or pornography, and that's not my suggestion here. Rather, we need to understand that God rejoices in the beautiful ways a husband and wife are enamored with and aroused by each other. And we need to celebrate that.

Relax.

Smile.

Sex is good.

Sex is *designed* to be good. Like so much of the poetry found in this book, sex is meant to be breathtaking and pleasurable. While some scholars suggest that Song of Solomon is intended as a metaphor for the love Christ has for the church, a second camp believes these verses comprise a literal love letter between a man and his wife.

I think we'll see in the next purpose—the ultimate purpose—it can be both.

The Ultimate Purpose of Sex: To Bring Glory to God

In everything we do, we are to glorify God with our actions. First Corinthians even says to do the most ordinary activities—eating and drinking—for God's glory. "For you have been bought with a price: therefore glorify God in your body . . . Whether, then, you eat or drink or whatever you do, do all to the glory of God" (1 Cor. 6:20; 10:31 NASB).

In the simplest acts of our lives, we are free in Christ to choose what we do, and because of that freedom we are called to do everything for the glory of God. Does that mean we're to have sex for the glory of God too? Yes. And if that sounds a little weird to you, you're not alone.

The messages we receive about sex—*some churches say it's dirty, some people say it's only for reproduction, today's culture says it's only for pleasure*—leave us grappling with conflicting information. I know married couples, like my friend Amy and her husband, who have grown up in the church or were raised in religious families and struggle with feelings of guilt when they have sex. Sometimes they experience this guilt only on their wedding night, but often it lasts for the duration of their marriage.

Sadly, because sex has been so distorted since Adam and Eve sinned in Eden, we must both acknowledge *and* fight the lies we're tempted to believe about it. The beautiful truth is that, in addition to procreation, consummation, and even pleasure, God created sex with *his* ultimate and final purpose in mind: to glorify him.

Paul specifically wrote about glorifying God with our bodies and sexuality in his first letter to the Corinthians. He addressed the Corinthian church, which began strong but, because of external cultural influences, ultimately strayed from God's design, especially in regard to his plan for sex. In particular, Paul addressed the Corinthian church leaders, who were engaging in sexual acts with prostitutes. He informed them of the physical and spiritual dangers of sex outside of marriage.

> Do you not know that your bodies are members of Christ? Shall I then take away the members of Christ and make them members of a prostitute? May it never be! Or do you not know that the one who joins himself to a prostitute is one body with her? For He says, "THE TWO SHALL BECOME ONE FLESH." But the one who joins himself to the Lord is one spirit *with* Him. Flee immorality. Every other sin that a man commits is outside the body, but the immoral man sins against his own body. Or do you not know that your body is a temple of the Holy Spirit who is in you, whom you have from God, and that you are not your own? For you have been bought with a price: *therefore glorify God in your body.*
>
> 1 Corinthians 6:15–20 NASB, emphasis added

Paul's words carry much gravity. It may appear as if he's saying sexual sin is worse than other sins. He's not. Instead, he is communicating *how* the consequences are different. All sins have consequences. Some sins hurt us, others cause pain to those around us, but Paul says sexual sin affects us, others, *and* God. I remember hearing a youth pastor tell his youth group that out of all the sins mentioned in the Bible, sexual sin is the only one we're told to flee from. Run from it. Fast.

In 1 Corinthians 6:16, you can see where Paul quotes Genesis 2:24. In Genesis, becoming "one flesh" means having sex. When the men in the Corinthian church have sex with a prostitute, Paul reminds them that in that sexual act, they unite with that woman in a way that is intended only for a man and his wife. Because they were "bought with a price" (the blood Christ shed for them on the cross), they are bringing an unholy act to the temple of God—their bodies, their minds, and their spirit.

Any sex that occurs outside of marriage has the same consequence Paul wrote about to the Corinthian church. But all is not lost in this sexual brokenness, which is not really anything different than we see and experience today. Paul doesn't end there and say, "Hey, you've sinned. That's it. You're done."

Having sex outside of marriage doesn't push God away from us. God loves us no matter what—no matter how egregious our sins and no matter how far we have turned from his plans, his wisdom, and his instruction for our lives. We are told in Romans 8:35 that *nothing* can separate us from God's love.

Much like Jesus told (and loved) the woman caught in adultery to "go and sin no more" (John 8:11), Paul writes, "Therefore glorify God in your body."

Sin no more. Rejoice! You're forgiven! You can choose now to glorify God with your body.

Your children will undoubtedly ask you questions about sex. A basic understanding of what Scripture says about God's purposes for sex will ultimately help you more clearly discern the best answers to your children's questions. We can trust that God didn't create something as powerful and intimate as sex and then abandon us to navigate our understanding of it, both for ourselves and for our children, on our own. He's given us fundamental truth in his Word that we can rely on when questions arise.

A Word about Your Own Past

We need to address something important before moving on to chapter 1: this discussion of sexuality may not be just about your children. You've picked up a book about how to navigate the process of talking to your kids about sex, but perhaps you're feeling a little bit ashamed or guilty. Perhaps the topics of sex, media, pornography, and abuse hit close to home—for not only your kids and how you communicate with them about such topics *but also for you.*

If we look at recent statistics, it's safe to say that more than half the people who read this book, men *and* women, struggle with some sort of brokenness related to sexuality. Perhaps you were abused. Maybe you grew up in a home that distorted the definition of sex, and now you're confused and harboring a wealth of questions. Perhaps you had sexual boundaries in place that were broken by others, or yourself, and now you are full of regret and remorse and unable to make peace with your past. Or maybe you've tried to stop looking at (or reading or watching) pornography and simply can't.

Are you carrying some kind of weight—a burden, a secret, a question, or shame—you just can't shake? Are you wondering how you're supposed to talk to your kids about purity when your past is full of mistakes or you can't seem to find a healthy sense of sexuality in your own life? (Side note: In using the word *purity*, I mean more than the standard "not having sex until you're married." Purity is equal parts what's above your waist and what's below it. It's mind, body, *and* spirit.)

It's okay.

Really, it is.

You don't have to wait for wholeness in your own life to talk to your kids about sex. You don't have to have a perfect past to talk honestly with your kids today. If you're delaying the conversation until you feel you're ready, as the adage says, "you'll never be ready." You need to accept your humanity, confess your shortcomings to God and others, and take action to get help *while* leading your family to become more aware and better equipped to fight these battles.

I'll never forget something my friend Jenny (who's a musician) said to me over coffee one day. We weren't talking about kids and sex, but the lesson still fits our discussion here. Jenny and I were talking about our current callings. Both of us spend a lot of time on the road, traveling, speaking, and ministering all over the country. Our husbands are entirely supportive of this, and most of the time they travel and minister alongside us. However, when Jenny was pregnant, she began to wonder how she could travel, minister, *and* be a mom. How could she leave her baby behind?

At one event, a very pregnant Jenny waddled off stage after she sang, her hand over her womb and her face awash in tears. She felt so conflicted about having to give up the thing she felt called to do with her gifts in order to fulfill her calling to be a mom. The event's headlining musician, Natalie, saw the look on Jenny's face, embraced her, and then, looking Jenny dead in the eyes, asked her two questions:

"Do you feel called to sing and minister and travel?"

Jenny said, "Yes."

"Do you feel called to be a mom?"

Looking down at her protruding belly, Jenny laughed a little as she said, "I hope so."

"God doesn't give you two conflicting callings, Jenny," Natalie said. "He can't. If you know you're called to minister on the road *and* you know you're called to be a mom, then you need to depend on him to show you how to do both. Trust him with this. I have. It's not been easy, but it's been true."

Jenny took Natalie's words to heart and, after taking a few months off to adjust to motherhood, resumed touring with her husband and her daughter. In fact, her daughter—at seven years old—now has elite status on an airline.

My point is this: if you're a parent, then God has called you to parent. Yet God also calls you to be whole and healed and complete in him. You can guide your children through wise decisions, *and* you can find freedom from shame or guilt, past or present. Your call to be holy and your call to nurture and protect as a parent do not contradict. *They can't*. It's not either/or. It's both.

"Your sexual mistakes are a unique opportunity to educate your own children," says Luke Gilkerson, education resource manager at Covenant Eyes, an internet accountability and filtering service. "Those mistakes don't make you ill-equipped. Past mistakes position you to speak from valuable experience and give you the ability to model what repentance looks like. Many parents mistakenly assume their authority to teach and guide rests on a clean track record. It doesn't. Instead, relish the opportunity to be transparent, to allow God to redeem your past by giving your kids the broad shoulders of your experiences on which to stand."

Don't believe the voices in your head that say you can't do both, the voices that tell you you're a hypocrite if you warn your kids to stay away from the things that have tempted you (or presently tempt you). Those voices are deceptive. They lie. The enemy is using them to inhibit both your freedom and your child's future.

Rhett Smith, a licensed therapist specializing in family and adolescent behavior, says, "I encourage parents not to let their own mistakes be a hindrance to having these conversations. Being honest with your kids will create a level of authentic vulnerability and connection that will help produce opportunities in the future for these tough conversations to emerge. Plus, there is a way to be honest about mistakes, while still having boundaries in your conversation and not glorifying the past."

You may feel like the least credible source to speak into your child's life, but because you are their parent, *you are inherently the most credible source.*

If you are currently struggling with sexual compulsions or wrestling with issues from the past, I urge you to get help. I'll refrain from offering a lot of specific advice here in order to stay focused on the central topic at hand, but please know that your child's freedom, health, and livelihood in this matter depend at least in part on your own freedom, health, and livelihood. I'll touch on this matter again in subsequent chapters. I've also included an extensive list of reading recommendations for you in the Resources for the Conversation section at the end of the book.

▶ THE BOTTOM LINE

I realize this section is overwhelming in some ways. You picked up a book looking for advice on how to talk with your kids about sex, and I've shared some things you maybe didn't expect. Although I've spent a lot of time with students in the last decade, I've easily spent twice as much time with adults. The responses I get from adults aren't any different from the ones I get from students: "I'm stuck." "I'm confused." "I need help." "I need hope." "I need to be free."

It's my prayer that you now realize hope and freedom are possible. As a person who has walked the road from struggle and dependence to healing and recovery, I promise that there is hope. There is freedom. And, equally important, I pray you know that no matter what your sexual stumbling blocks are—past or present—*you* are the most qualified person to talk to your child about sex.

EXPERTS WANT YOU TO KNOW

Dr. Russell D. Moore is president of the Ethics & Religious Liberty Commission of the Southern Baptist Convention, the moral concerns and public policy entity of the nation's largest Protestant denomination. He is a frequent cultural commentator, an ethicist, a theologian, and an ordained Southern Baptist minister. The *Wall Street Journal* has called him "vigorous, cheerful, and fiercely articulate," while the Gospel Coalition has referred to him as "one of the most astute ethicists in contemporary evangelicalism." Moore is the author of several books, including *Onward: Engaging the Culture without Losing the Gospel*. A native Mississippian, Dr. Moore and his wife, Maria, are the parents of five sons.

Why is it difficult for the Christian culture, generally speaking, to acknowledge the beauty of sex as described in Scripture?

I wouldn't agree that every wing of Christian culture finds it difficult to describe the beauty of sexuality. Some sectors do so quite well. It is true, though, that many sectors fall short. Some of those reasons are cultural, but I think many are intrinsic to the nature of sexuality itself. Sexuality is, by definition, mysterious—pointing beyond itself to the cosmic union of Christ and the church (Eph. 5). Moreover, sexuality is, by definition, veiled in a certain degree of privacy—within the marital union. When these truths are added to a kind of idolization of sex within the world around us, navigating the balance of emphasizing the beauty of sex while respecting its mystery can become difficult.

Not everyone reading this book—its author included—has followed God's plan for biblical sexuality perfectly. How can we acknowledge and accept that although past mistakes may have consequences, God still wants us to experience his gift of sex to the fullest?

Jesus said the healthy don't need a doctor, but the sick do. The gospel is only good news to sinners. A gospel view of sexuality means a view of sexuality from the cross, and in the cross we see both the full justice and the full mercy of God. Those who excuse past sexual sin as meaningless once they are married have not truly repented. Fornication, like adultery, is infidelity—infidelity to God, infidelity to one's future spouse, and infidelity to the community of faith. A marriage can be healed, and even thrive, after adultery, but someone who takes lightly their past adultery will not be able to reconcile and move forward. The same is true for other forms of sexual sin. Sexual immorality is not just bad for us temporally. Sexual immorality splits us apart from one another and, if not addressed, will damn us. The good news is that, in the cross, Jesus took on the curse and exile due to sinners, including sexual sinners, in fullness. This means repentant sinners are not only forgiven but also joined to and hidden in Christ so that his life becomes their life, his history their history. That's good news.

How do we know that what the biblical authors wrote centuries ago about sex still applies to our culture today?

I don't really agree that culture has changed all that dramatically in regard to sex. Sexual immorality is present everywhere in the biblical story line and was omnipresent in many of the ancient cultures in Scripture. The strategies for rationalizing sexual rebellion change, and the taboos switch from generation to generation, but the root issue is always the same.

Human beings don't want to be creatures. We want to be like gods or like animals. We want to be accountable only to ourselves, including in the naming of what's good and evil. And we want to be driven by our own appetites, at least part of the time. That hasn't changed and won't until the eschaton.

The biblical writers, in and of themselves, aren't able to speak to our culture, or to any culture, on sex or anything else. They are only able to do so if they are speaking—like the biblical authors claim they are—by the Spirit of God. That's the question. Our first question is one of authority: "Has God really said . . . ?" If God deposited his revelation through the writings of prophets and apostles, then the Bible is his Word to us. We don't depend, then, on the personal expertise of the prophets and apostles but on their prophetic inspiration.

Without that prophetic inspiration, all we have are the culturally bound perspectives of first-century Middle Eastern men. Why listen to that? But if God, through these men, is actually speaking truth for all of human history, then we better listen.

1

The Earlier, the Better

Talking to Your Kids about Sex

When it comes to parents talking to their kids about sex (including porn, the media, sexual abuse, masturbation, et al.), the most common question I hear again and again is when parents should start the discussion.

When's the right time? When's too early? Is it too late? How much do I share? When do I share?

Here's the good news: you don't need to have "the talk" with your child. Let's shelve that dreaded conversation about the birds and the bees now and forever . . . and ever. Amen.

I'd like to take a moment to make something very clear. If there's one thing you need to remember from this book, it's this: Talking to your kids about sex is *not* a onetime event. It is an ongoing conversation.

You'll talk to your kids about various aspects of sexuality from the time they're in diapers, through their elementary school and teenage years and, yes, even into adulthood.

Therapist Rhett Smith encourages parents to see these conversations as ongoing.

> The days of the onetime "birds and bees" talk is long gone. And if we wait to have that onetime talk, we have most likely missed important opportunities along the way to engage our kids in conversations. Plus, it eases the pressure on parents to have all the answers when they know there will be ongoing conversations, rather than one shot. I encourage parents not only to begin these conversations early, since some studies show (as does my experience with clients) that the average age of exposure to pornography is somewhere between five and nine, but also, as kids progress developmentally, to have ongoing conversations.

We must stop seeing sex as shameful, awkward, and embarrassing. Can these conversations be a little uncomfortable? Absolutely. But sex, in and of itself, is beautiful and should be celebrated as the good and perfect gift God has intended it to be. When we're excited about something, we want to talk to others about it. And we should be excited about sex!

Repeat after me: *we should be excited about sex!*

Doctors and psychologists have researched how a child's brain matures and develops. If you have children, then you know when to expect certain milestones—rolling over, teething, saying a first word, crawling, and walking. As your children get older, they are able to understand more and more, which is why initiating age-appropriate conversations about sex as early as possible is the key to making these conversations a normal and expected part of family life.

In *The Focus on the Family® Guide to Talking with Your Kids about Sex*,[1] the Physicians Resource Council breaks down the "when" and the "how much" according to different age groups, each with unique developmental needs. This book is a great read if you're looking for more material on topics other than (but still related to) sex (like anatomy, physical changes boys and girls experience through childhood and the teen years, and other medical information relating to sex). For the purposes of this book, we'll stick to the basics of what to talk about and when regarding sex, as well as the most common issues and questions related to each age group.

Having the Conversation

As you learn about which conversation points are appropriate for each age group and make plans to begin and continue your discussion, keep in mind your family values. If you're wondering about the best way to address a particular idea with your child, refer back to these, pray, and discuss the question with your spouse or a trusted friend:

Family Values

- We believe God created sex to be a worshipful experience between husband and wife that brings glory to him.
- We believe that because we live in a fallen world and will constantly face distorted views of sexuality, we must learn to identify and process these views in a healthy and biblically sound manner.
- We believe in honest conversation, even if it feels uncomfortable, antiquated, or old-fashioned.
- We believe everybody is created in God's image, and no one should be abused or exploited for any reason.
- We believe we should not be ashamed of sex or sexuality— ever.

- We believe in showing grace, mercy, and love in every circumstance, even toward people whose beliefs we don't agree with or understand.
- We believe in the healing and redemptive power of the love of God, who sacrificed his Son, Jesus Christ, for our sins.
- We believe in having integrity in our thoughts, words, and actions by demonstrating God's love to everyone, including ourselves, regardless of past or present circumstances.
- We believe in asking for help when we need it.
- We believe in relying on the power of God and prayer, as well as being accountable to our family and friends when we struggle.

Age Group 1: Infants to Four-Year-Olds[2]

While you won't be talking to your infant about sex, your actions will help establish a healthy connection and attachment with your child, even at this very young age. Believe it or not, a child's sexual development begins at birth. During these tender formative years, your child begins to learn about love and identity. Your warm, caring touch is helping to form neural pathways in their brain. Your child is learning to trust you. They hear your voice, recognize your face, and know your touch. They learn to count on you to protect them.

Once infants become aware of their bodies, one of their favorite activities is to play with their genitals. While we know this isn't a sexual experience for them, it feels good nonetheless. If you're in public and want your child to stop touching themselves, distract them with something else fun (and if possible, something tactile). It's important not to shame your child for their behavior. It's purely innocent—there's nothing to be ashamed of!

As children begin to listen more attentively and speak, it's normal for parents to point out and identify body parts, such as eye, ear, nose, and mouth. This is a great way to introduce your child to his penis or her vagina or vulva. Often parents use other words like *wee-wee* or *hoo-hoo*, and while there's nothing wrong with this per se, by using the correct anatomical terms, you will be communicating to your child that there's nothing concerning their bodies to be embarrassed about.

As you enter the potty training phase, most doctors think it's okay to continue using whatever slang is common (e.g., *pee* or *potty* or *poop*). Just make sure you also offer your child the proper terms, such as *urinate* or *bowel movement*. Using formal terms facilitates overall communication and establishes a clear standard vocabulary for future conversations.

As toddlers head into the preschool years, they begin to comprehend at a more sophisticated developmental level, which means it's a good time to initiate the conversation about "good touch" and "bad touch." Explain to your child how important it is for them to tell you if anyone touches their genitals or if someone asks your child to touch theirs. Offer your child concrete examples that are easily understandable.

For instance, explain that if mom is giving you a bath, that's "good touch." Or if a doctor is examining you with dad in the room, that's okay too. But make sure your child recognizes that if anyone else touches or asks to touch them, it would be considered "bad touch" (even if it feels good), and you, as their parent or guardian, need to be told about it right away.

You might want to consider having a conversation about "secrets" like my friends Laura and Josh have had with their two small children. "If someone tells you to keep a secret, even from your mom and dad," Laura and Josh explained to their kids, "promise us that you won't. You'll never get in trouble for telling us your secret."

Even though they're only three and five years old, Laura and Josh's kids have heard that message reinforced so many times that they know when they hear a secret, they tell. I learned this when I asked their son not to tell when I snuck a piece of pepperoni off of his pizza. "It'll be our little secret!" I said and was immediately ratted out.

The preschool years are also the perfect age to explain to your child which acts need to be kept private, like going to the bathroom or touching their genitals. If you're in public and see your child with their hand down their pants, instead of harshly punishing or correcting them (because that would be shaming), explain that you understand it feels good when they touch and explore their own body, but it should not be done in public places. Don't get frustrated. You're going to have this conversation *a lot*. A mom of a young boy once told me she and her son have this conversation over and over. "Boys seem to have a heightened fascination with their penis. Even as babies. The diaper comes off and their hands go to their penis," she said.

Children in this age group are curious. Don't be shocked to hear the questions "Why?" and "How?" more frequently as they get older. It's unlikely they'll ask about sex at this age, but just in case, ask your child, "What do you mean?"

By asking your child to explain what they mean when they ask a question, you're doing two things. First, you're not giving them an answer they're not ready to hear. And second, you find out what they know. For example, if your son asks, "Where do babies come from?" instead of explaining sexual intercourse, ask him, "What do you mean?" He may respond by saying, "Jimmy said babies come from Santa Claus. Did I come from Santa?" You can answer his question directly. "No, you didn't come from Santa. You came from a special place inside of me called the womb (or the uterus). All mommies have one where babies stay safe and warm and grow."

In any instance, it's critical not to humiliate or threaten your child in any way during this formative age. If you're in the store and your son is touching his penis, don't slap his hand away and say, "If you keep playing with your wee-wee, it's going to fall off!" Sadly, parents often react this way.

▶ **THE BOTTOM LINE**

In the infant to four-year-old age group especially, focus on connecting, accepting, answering questions appropriately, and never shaming.

Age Group 2: Early Elementary School[3]

When I was eight years old, my family moved to a small town outside San Angelo, Texas. As we carried in boxes with a group of friends from our new church, we realized my five-year-old brother was missing. After looking all around the house and in the backyard, we opened his bedroom closet door. My brother and a girl his age were sitting on the closet floor lip-locked in a kiss.

Being the older, wiser sibling, I screamed, "Mom!" and began chanting the infamous song, "Paul and Amber sitting in a tree. K-I-S-S-I-N-G." My mother came into the room and said, "Paul! What *are* you doing?" Amber, his little "girlfriend," said, "We're kissing. Duh."

As children enter their early elementary years, their social circles expand, as does their curiosity about sex and their bodies. Although an understanding of modesty begins to take root (wanting to undress or bathe alone), boys and girls also become curious about what makes them boys and girls.

Encouraging modesty at this age is another important developmental step. If you have children of the opposite sex who share a room, make sure there are boundaries in place that allow them their own private space to undress. This is also the age when most doctors agree that mixed-gender baths or showers should end.

My brother isn't the only one in my family with an embarrassing kissing story. When I was in first grade, we had movie time every Friday in school. The two first-grade classes would join together and sit on a rug in one of the rooms to watch a cartoon. Most times a boy from the other class sat behind me. One Friday, he tapped me on the shoulder.

"Hey. I'll give you a gold necklace if you kiss me."

Are you kidding me? Gold? I told him yes, gave him a quick peck on the lips, and quickly turned back around. He attended my birthday party a few weeks later and, sure enough, gave me a necklace with a small gold butterfly embellished with a fake pearl. I actually still have the pendant in a keepsake box.*

Before you deem my mom and dad unfit parents, especially for a pastor and his wife, please understand that the type of behavior my brother and I exhibited, although sexual in *nature*, wasn't sexual in *intent*. A child's brain at this age is not developed enough to know or understand sexual arousal or satisfaction. Rather, this is an experimental mirroring stage.

*My husband thinks this is weird.

Children often mimic the behavior and actions they see in the media or in public. They are also beginning to say their first curse words simply because they've heard others say them. They likely don't know what they really mean. Similarly, "playing doctor" is a common game among children in early elementary school. If you learn your child has exposed themselves or asked another child to do so, it's an opportunity for education, not necessarily a cause for concern (unless this happens repeatedly despite your instruction).

Simply ask your child, calmly, "Why were you and your friend naked?" As long as they weren't trying to have sex or one did not force the other to participate, take this opportunity to discuss why we keep our bodies private and how we should be naked only by ourselves, never with a friend. If possible, try and involve the other child's parents so that they can communicate with their own child. Let them know what happened and see if you can both agree about how to approach the situation with your children.

Children this age also hear more from the media and from their friends at school than we realize. As a result, your kids might begin to ask more specific questions about where babies come from, or what "sex" or "making love" means. Don't feel like you need to give a doctoral dissertation about it. This age group doesn't have the attention span or ability to remember particular details. Offer them something very basic like, "When a mommy and a daddy feel a special type of love for each other, they go somewhere private, undress, and the daddy puts his penis inside the mommy's vagina. It feels very good for both of them." Let them know this is a special gift God has given a husband and a wife after they are married. Reinforce that, as a child, it is not something they are supposed to do (but one day when they're older and married, they will!). Ask your child to repeat your explanation back to you, just so you can make sure they understand what you're communicating, and you can clear up anything they misheard or misunderstood.

To end this on a light note, my neighbor-friend Amy, whom I mentioned earlier, recently shared this amusing story about how her seven-year-old son, Jack, understood the age-old question of where babies come from:

> I've never actually discussed how babies are formed, but when Jack asked me how the baby comes out, he couldn't understand the idea of a vaginal delivery. He thought, even after I explained everything, that women "pooped them out." Having something leave the tummy in his mind meant poop. I can't wait until he reads this book when he's older.

▶ THE BOTTOM LINE

Children in early elementary school are curious. It's important to encourage and engage their questions, clarify what they are really asking or what they've really heard, and then answer their questions succinctly and appropriately. As we discussed earlier, don't shame or dismiss your child for exploring their body. Instead, help them understand appropriate touch and boundaries and the importance of privacy and modesty.

Age Group 3: Older Elementary School and Early Middle School[4]

I hate to tell you this, but your baby isn't your baby anymore.

This is a time of incredible transition and growth, and you are going to see it happen *fast*. Your child's independence begins to form quickly during this time. As a parent, this may be a particularly difficult (though wonderfully beautiful) time for you as you witness your child grow and mature. It's essential to ensure they understand basic anatomy and the function of sex and reproduction. Why?

Because puberty is about to blow through your house with its hormonal hurricane-force power.

(And you need to prepare your kids . . . *now*.)

Puberty, the process of a young person's sexual organs maturing so they become capable of reproducing, generally takes place between the ages of nine and eleven but sometimes hits sooner . . . or later. My mom, who teaches third grade, has seen children as young as seven begin to menstruate and develop breasts. However, I didn't really hit puberty until right before I graduated from high school. I was the only girl in my class who didn't begin menstruation until later in my teens.*

The sooner you talk to your kids about what to expect during puberty, the better. They should be old enough to understand basic anatomical terms and the definition of sex. Even though it can feel incredibly odd, using a book with illustrations (not real-life photographs) that explain the physical developments that take place during puberty can be helpful in showing your child the changes they can expect. With the many books available online and in bookstores, I'm certain you can find one that suits your needs and reflects your values. If you can't find something that works, talk to your child's pediatrician for advice and resources, or visit 5ThingsBook.com.

*I told you I was going to make this uncomfortable.

Around this age, schools often introduce sex education or puberty education into the curriculum. Usually the school requests parental permission for the child to participate in the class, but that isn't always the case. I never had a formal sex education class, but I distinctly recall that around the age of ten or eleven, my small class was separated by gender into two different rooms. I don't know what the boys' class did, but in the girls' class, we watched a video about menstruation and, afterward, our teacher passed around various maxi pads and tampons so we could see how they worked. Since I was pretty clueless about my anatomy, the thought of using a tampon was fairly traumatic for me (which is probably why I remember it so vividly now, almost thirty years later!). Don't hesitate to ask your child's school about their policy for teaching *anything* about sexuality. Ask to review the materials. If it's not common practice for the school to ask for parents' permission, help other parents understand what is being taught and, if necessary, encourage the school to implement a parental permission-based policy for all sexual education.

After she knew her son went through a sex ed class at his school, Diane, the mother of an eleven-year-old boy, asked him at dinner, "So did you learn anything from that film you watched in school today? What did you think?" Her question shows that talking about sex is as normal as eating spaghetti on a Tuesday night. The conversation may not be any less uncomfortable, but it's progressing. I'll share a little bit more in detail about sex ed in the next section.

Kids this age also tend to talk about having a girlfriend or boyfriend. My first official boyfriend was in my gifted and talented class in the third grade (he was a fourth grader too!). He simply asked if I wanted to be his girlfriend. I said yes. I doodled his name on my notebooks, and once, on a field trip, we secretly held hands. I remember feeling excited—though not sexually aroused—by our relationship. For the record, we never broke up. The following summer, I moved away and assumed I would never see him again. For what it's worth, that assumption was incorrect, as he and I attended the same church camp seven years later!

My husband, Tim, also found his first girlfriend in the third grade. We'll call her Jill. A group of Jill's friends approached Tim on the playground and said, "Jill likes you. Do you want to be her boyfriend?" Tim simply said, "Okay." Three days later, the same group of friends returned. "Jill wants to break up with you because you never talk to her." Again, Tim replied, "Okay."

Serious relationships, boyfriends and girlfriends as we think of them, likely aren't going to develop during this age. Instead, their relationships are a mirroring of what they see happening in culture or with older siblings and family members. However, don't ignore these innocent mentions. When you start to hear the words *boyfriend* and *girlfriend* as part of your child's vocabulary, it's the perfect time to start talking about . . .

(Take a deep breath . . .)

(One more time . . .)

Dating.

Don't worry, you're not going to send your nine-year-old out for dinner and a movie with the boy who sits behind her in class, but the earlier you start talking about dating, *when the time comes*, the message already will have been well received. We'll touch on dating a little more in the next section, but for now, view these conversations as opportunities to continue reinforcing your open-door policy about all things preadolescent.

Another topic you should explore* with your kids at this age is masturbation (we'll talk more about this topic as it relates to the next age group as well). I first heard about masturbation (the act, not the term) in the fifth grade, so I was about ten or eleven years old. A girl in my class told me she learned that if she put her fingers "up there" (in her vagina), it felt really good.

I was scared out of my mind.

That night, I started crying so hard my mom came into my room. I told her I couldn't sleep, and after about thirty minutes of her sitting on the bed with me, I told her what I had learned at school. I was afraid because I thought everyone was doing this scary thing and that I should be doing it too. I don't remember what she said in response, but I know she didn't shame me for having questions or learning about it. I do, however, remember that she told me if I had any more questions, I could always ask her.†

▶ THE BOTTOM LINE

Talking about puberty, boyfriends and girlfriends, modesty, and masturbation is going to be really uncomfortable for both you and your child. Godspeed. You'll do fine. If you need some prayer beforehand, shoot me an email. In all seriousness, though, this is an important developmental age for your child. Keep the lines of communication open during this critical time and save any shocked reactions for a private moment.

*No pun intended . . .
†My mom is super cool.

Age Group 4: Middle School and Younger High School[5]

Welcome to the beginning of the end. I'm just kidding. But if you have a child in this age group, you know what I mean. Changes are happening, and they're happening fast. Get ready for Jekyll and Hyde.

At this point you've probably talked with your child a bit about the physical changes that accompany puberty and covered the basics of sex. Now it's time to talk about lots and lots of topics.

Dating

I realize it may seem too early to talk about dating, but your child is in junior high now. Puberty is likely in full swing, and boys and girls are taking notice of each other.

I don't think there's a one-size-fits-all answer to the question, "When should my child date?" That's completely up to your family. My parents allowed me to go on my first date at the age of thirteen. His mom drove us to the mall where we saw *Jurassic Park* at the theater. Then she picked us up after the movie and drove me home. We probably held hands and, although I don't remember, it wouldn't surprise me if we kissed.

For me, this was not the end of the world. I didn't start sleeping around, stuffing my bra, or wearing skintight clothes.* I think I was stricter with myself in my dating relationships and what I considered holy (and wise) physically as a single adult than my parents were with me as a teen. This isn't my parents' fault. They told me what was acceptable in dating. They explained that it was okay to kiss a boy if I wanted to, and it was also okay to say no. I stayed within those boundaries pretty well.

*Confession: I may have stuffed my bra once or twice.

My only suggestion for all parents regarding dating is that you have a two-way conversation with your child about dating *before they date*. Ask them what their thoughts are and what dating means to them. Together, create some boundaries and set expectations. They'll feel ownership and responsibility and will be more likely to respond well as situations arise. Most important, discuss the "why" behind the conversation. Remember that everything, including dating, points back to the glory of God. Don't be shy about encouraging them to ask, "By doing this (dating, kissing, etc.), are we bringing glory to God?"

Just the other night after a youth group outing, I sat in my car with two seventh-grade girls. As we waited for their parents to pick them up, one of them asked, "What do you think about dating at our age?" Clearly, the topic of dating is very near and dear to these young and tender hearts.

Oral Sex

By this time, your child should have a correct understanding of what sexual intercourse is and how babies are made. And if you haven't done so already, it's time to talk about oral sex.*

Scientific data on oral sex and middle schoolers is almost nonexistent, and, in a way, I understand why. No one wants to believe these young children are performing oral sex on one another. If you were to research it, you'd find stories, but the statistics are few and far between. High schoolers, however, have been well researched. If you want to prepare your middle school children for the kind of pressures high school will bring (and middle school likely brings), talking about oral sex now is key.

*I will give you a moment to catch your breath and let your heart rate decrease.

A study by the United States Centers for Disease Control and Prevention says that

> based on the National Survey of Family Growth (NSFG) data from 2006–2008, 45% of females and 48% of males aged 15–19 years had ever had oral sex with members of the opposite sex, and among 20–24 year-olds, these percentages were about 81% of females and 80% of males.[6]

Most teens who engage in oral sex do so because they are prolonging their "technical" virginity (i.e., avoiding sexual intercourse) while maintaining social and peer status.[7] They don't think oral sex is "real" sex.

What does this mean? The short answer: a lot of kids are having oral sex.

A story reported in an Indiana newspaper reads,

> For one in four abstinent teens, oral sex is the solution. . . . Oral sex is . . . culturally the new good night kiss.[8]

Another story from clinical psychologist Dr. Sharon Maxwell says that

> one of the few surveys done nationally, a 2000 poll by *Seventeen Magazine*, found that 55 percent of teens responding reported they'd had oral sex and 40 percent didn't consider it sex.[9]

Wow. Is your heart palpitating? Mine is. It just doesn't seem right to be talking to our middle schoolers about oral sex . . . but it's necessary now. It really is. And keep in mind that these surveys were conducted *decades ago*. With the introduction of the internet, social media, and other cultural influences, kids now have access to more sexually explicit information at a much younger age. Chances are that they know more than you think they do. In the end, it's better for this kind of information to come from you than from their peers or the media and the web (we'll address this more specifically in chapter 4: "Google Is the New Sex Ed").

Right now you might be asking yourself, *How do I do this? How do I bring up the topic of oral sex with my kids?* Dr. Claire McCarthy, MD, from Boston Children's Hospital, offers these great (and simple) talking points:

- Sexual feelings are normal. You shouldn't feel bad for having them.
- That said, sex can have consequences. You can get sick or pregnant, and it can change how you feel about yourself and how others think about you. You need to understand those consequences. (Parent can ad lib here and talk more about those consequences, based on their kid's level of understanding.)
- Oral sex is sex. It's not like kissing. You can't get pregnant, but you can still get infections. And it can still affect how you feel about yourself and how others think about you. Not only that, it can lead to other kinds of sex. (If parent has the fortitude, they can talk about other kinds of sex.)
- It's your body and your life. Don't let anyone make you do something you don't want to do (and conversely, don't ever try to make anyone do something they don't want to do).
- *And there's one other thing you should say, because it really is the point*: I can't promise you that I won't be upset if you have sex. But I can promise you that I will always love you, no matter what.[10]

This is not getting any easier, is it? I'm sorry. Please remember that you are brave. You've got this. God's got this. Let's keep moving. We still have a long way to go.

Date Rape

Another topic to consider discussing at this age is date rape. Really? Should you be concerned at this age? Should you be concerned at all?

I say, yes. Here's why. In a recent Facebook discussion in which I talked about teens and dating, one commenter on my author's page said this:

> I talk pretty regularly with my thirteen-year-old daughter about adult topics, including sex. The other day I thought it was a little odd that we talked about Rohypnol and the situations where that might be an issue, but after she went to school and discussed it with friends—they all knew about it. I was glad she heard about something from me first. That got me thinking; maybe hearing about sex and related topics from me first is the best plan.

You might be asking yourself, *How do I initiate a conversation about date rape with my child?* It's not easy. If you can, find a relatively recent news story about an incident involving date rape (unfortunately, this shouldn't be too difficult) and talk to your child about how to protect themselves. Discuss alcohol, drugs, and peer pressure. Let your child know they can call you at any time, no matter where they are or what they are doing, without judgment from you. Remind your kids that you always have their best interests in mind and that, because you love them, you are always available for them. Thinking of date rape at this age is a scary thing, both for you and for your child. By addressing it now, in a controlled environment, you can help shape how your child responds to situations in the future.

Masturbation

Masturbation isn't mentioned in the Bible, but within the overall Protestant evangelical belief system, there are generally three beliefs[11] about the "morality" of masturbation:

1. It's totally normal and acceptable.
2. It's totally normal but not acceptable.
3. It's totally normal but acceptable only if a person does not commit the sin of lust.

When parents (or students) email or ask me in person if masturbation is a sin, I generally ask *why* they want to know. Most people confess they feel guilty after they masturbate. If it's appropriate, I then ask why they feel guilty. I want to make sure the person asking has a clear view of what God intends for us to experience sexually in marriage. If they say, "I shouldn't feel that way [aroused]," I encourage them to embrace the fact that God designed them to have feelings of arousal.

With that said, my beliefs fall largely into the third category (it's normal but can result from or include lust, which is a sin). On December 14, 2010, the elders and pastors at The Village Church in Dallas, Texas, penned, in my opinion, one of the best dissections of a "theology of masturbation." This summary (of a much longer piece found on the church's website) says:

It seems to the pastors and elders of The Village Church that masturbation is prohibited for a couple of reasons. First, we would prohibit the act based upon the provision of marriage as the only appropriate institution in which to express sexual intimacy. . . . Marriage is the gracious and holy prescription for sexual desire, the only prescription afforded by the Creator of all good desire. Second, we would counsel abstinence due to the overwhelming and innate relationship between masturbation and lust. Lust is extremely serious and not to be taken lightly, dismissed, or played with.

While we are cautious about universally calling all masturbation sinful in all instances, it seems abundantly clear to us that such a stance should be the default position. Pastorally, we would strongly recommend abstinence.[12]

Regardless of your personal or family's stance on masturbation, the one important rule to follow as you have these conversations is to let your child know they have no reason to be ashamed of their feelings and questions. It's important to note that God doesn't want us to *suppress* our innate sexual desires. Instead, he wants us to grow in the discipline of self-control.

Pornography

Finally, this age is also a good time to initiate an ongoing conversation about pornography, and it's time to prepare now. We'll explore this topic in greater detail in chapter 4, "Google Is the New Sex Ed." For now, I just wanted to give you a heads-up.

The Positive Influence of a Church Community

I realize everything you've read might feel a bit overwhelming and frightening, but take a deep breath. Research shows that children who are involved in religious activities or are committed to their faith are less likely to fall victim to peer pressure.[13]

Taylor, a young woman I know, is a great example of this. Before Taylor was really involved in church, she was the stereotypical teenage party girl—drinking on the weekends, hanging out with guys, and, as she puts it, "Just doing stupid stuff. All the time." After hitting her own rock bottom following a friend's suicide, Taylor realized she needed help and, as a result, became more active in her youth group and church. She also began to reach out to and connect with her parents more.

Taylor and her parents jumped deep into their faith, and just one year later, this girl is unshakeable. Her faith is strong, and although it hurts her to see her friends making some of the same mistakes she made, she loves them (yet doesn't allow them to influence her). It's been an honor to see her grow. I can't wait to see what God continues to do in her life. He truly works everything for the good, even when things seem scary (or hopeless).

▶ **THE BOTTOM LINE**

Your child undoubtedly knows more than you think they do. By now, you should be discussing puberty, dating, masturbation, sex, and pornography regularly with them. Remember, it's never too late to begin the conversation!

Age Group 5: High School and Beyond[14]

I know it may feel as if you're in the middle of a never-ending hormone zone, but I promise you, relief (and maturity) is just around the corner. Hormones are slowly stabilizing. And by now you should have covered at least the basics of gender differences, puberty, dating, and sexuality with your child.

Sex education doesn't stop. Schools aren't the only ones offering sex-ed classes. In late September 2015, actress Jessica Biel, along with WomanCare Global, launched a series of sex-ed videos for girls and women. I admire their desire to start (or continue) the conversation and empower women to be confident about their sexuality; however, they ask a poignant question with their campaign slogan: "If you don't tell them, who will?" If you're okay with Jessica talking to your kids about sex, maybe check it out. But I strongly encourage you, the guardian of your children, to be the one to start and continue these conversations.

While we're on the topic of sex ed, there are also "for teen, by teen" sites out there that encourage preteens and teens to educate themselves on sexuality. Again, I do appreciate the fact that people are willing to discuss sex freely . . . but I really think this conversation needs to land in the parents' realm of responsibility, regardless of their spiritual beliefs.

There is no shortage of these websites, as a quick internet search will prove. One of these sites is sexetc.org, which is published by Answer, a national organization that provides access to comprehensive sex education for young people and the adults who teach them. On the sexetc.org "About" page, the group notes that its mission is to improve teen sexual health by providing answers to teens' questions about sexually transmitted diseases, birth control, pregnancy, sexual orientation, and many other topics. The site includes stories written by teen staff writers, moderated forums, a state-by-state guide to teens' rights regarding sexual issues, as well as videos about sexual health and a glossary of approximately four hundred sex terms.

In its definition of "Abstinence-Until-Marriage Programs," Sex, Etc. refers to plans that use scare tactics to keep people from having sex until they are married with no balanced or unbiased view. So while the website may be extremely informational, the group doesn't communicate or even fairly explore the values a traditional Christian family believes and would teach.

But now you might want to consider talking to your kids about birth control. This doesn't mean you condone premarital sex. However, your child should know what birth control is. They should also be aware of the various types and the risks and benefits that go along with each one. They will hear about birth control somewhere. Wouldn't it be best if it were from you?

Now is also the time to educate your child about sexually transmitted diseases and abortion (even if your child has already learned about these topics at school and elsewhere). And, of course, continue the conversations about pornography, dating, and sex, remembering that it's important to keep the communication open and the dialogue flowing. The work you've done in the earlier years should pay off now, as your child is accustomed to talking with you about challenging topics and is not nearly as uncomfortable as they would be without that groundwork.

Many of today's high school students (and sometimes younger students as well) also wrestle with a question many of us didn't overtly confront at this age—is it wrong (or a sin) to be gay? I realize this is a polarizing topic, both in evangelical and political worlds, and my intent here is to speak as graciously but biblically as possible since this is a common question I get from high schoolers (and now, even some middle schoolers).

I admit that I don't have a lot of personal experience when it comes to same-sex attraction. In my late teens and early twenties, when I looked at pornography, I wondered why I enjoyed images of nude women as much as I did. I wondered why the pictures aroused me and whether my feelings meant that I was gay or bisexual. However, I knew I really, *really*, liked guys. As a result, I was extremely confused and ashamed to talk to anyone about this struggle.

Guess what? It turns out my feelings were normal and common. It's considered natural for some adolescents to have questions about or even experience same-sex attraction during their high school years.[15]

The church has hotly debated whether sexual orientation (being biologically predisposed to heterosexuality or homosexuality) is legitimate. In other words, is someone born straight? Is someone born gay? Is someone born bisexual? Asexual? Pansexual? As they have prayerfully considered both theology and scientific research, even some of the most conservative evangelical leaders have concluded that we are born with a specific sexual orientation and that orientation, in and of itself, is not sin.

For example, Dr. R. Albert Mohler Jr., president of the Southern Baptist Theological Seminary, recently said,

> I repented of denying the existence of sexual orientation because denying it was deeply confusing to people struggling with same-sex attraction. Biblical Christians properly resist any suggestion that our will can be totally separated from sexual desire, but we really do understand that the will is not a sufficient explanation for a pattern of sexual attraction. Put simply, most people experiencing a same-sex attraction tell of discovering it within themselves at a very early age, certainly within early puberty. As they experience it, a sexual attraction or interest simply "happens," and they come to know it.[16]

I have many friends who are gay. Some are celibate. Some are in same-sex relationships. Others are in mixed-orientation relationships (where they feel God's call to love and marry a straight person of the opposite sex and have children).

Most of my gay friends respect my understanding of theology on same-sex attraction. I do believe that some people are born attracted to the same sex. I believe some people are born biologically as a male or a female (having a penis or a vagina) but may feel like they're in the "wrong body" (gender expression). In my opinion, there is no one-size-fits-all answer on being oriented as gay, bisexual, nonsexual, transsexual, or pansexual. Many things influence one's sexual identity, including nature, nurture, or any or all combinations of these.

Each person who reads this book may very well have a differing view on same-sex attraction and gay relationships, but one thing is certain: homosexuality/bisexuality/transexuality is a topic we must discuss with our children. In the course of writing this book, two major current events transpired in regard to this topic that gained a lot of worldwide media attention: Bruce Jenner's transformation into becoming (physically) a woman, Caitlyn Jenner. Also, the Supreme Court's ruling that the US constitution recognizes the right to same-sex marriage. Because of the headlines, I am sure many kids were exposed to this dialogue.

Some teens may feel more comfortable and even attracted to someone of the same sex simply because they relate better to that specific person. This doesn't mean they're gay or bisexual or straight. I know it might be shocking to hear your child tell you they are attracted to the same sex. An announcement like this can cause a lot of confusion and even despair for families, particularly for Christians who believe that marriage is God's design for a man and a woman.

My first piece of advice is that you and your family turn to the Bible. It's important that you know what Scripture says about marriage and sexual activity outside of marriage. When your values have been established and communicated, the most important thing you can do if your child comes out to you (shares with you that they are gay/bi/trans/non/pan) is to love them. *Unconditionally*.

My friend Brian is in a mixed orientation marriage. He's identified as gay since he was in his teens. As he studied Scripture (he has a master's degree in biblical exegesis from Wheaton College Graduate School), he came to an understanding that God purposed him to be celibate or married to a woman.

In an interview I did with Brian about his mixed-orientation marriage, he said he was surprised to find himself physically, emotionally, relationally, and spiritually attracted to his then girlfriend. He explains:

> We got married for two very normal but important reasons. First, we were in love with each other in every way that one experiences love in the early days of a relationship. Second, we were convinced that we could help others better together than if we were apart. At our core, we knew God was bringing us together so that we could serve more effectively together. That formed the basis of our best hopes and expectations for our marriage. Looking back, we could never have imagined what this would blossom into through the years of smiles, trials, and pain.

Brian offers this advice on what to do if your teen expresses their attraction to people of the same sex:

It would not be fair of me to expect this short interview to completely reorient your understanding of sexuality, so I'm not going to try to do that. That's a journey worth taking, and some of you will be called to take it. But you don't need to have walked down that path to be the parent that your child needs when he or she makes the decision to come out as lesbian, gay, bisexual, transgender, or otherwise queer.

Maybe those words represent some of your worst fears as a parent. Perhaps they represent broken hopes and expectations for your family. You fear the social stigmas at church—where did your parenting go wrong where others did not? You wonder what this means for your son or daughter's relationship with God. You may even feel a new, deep anger and hurt toward God, your spouse, and your child, no matter how much you don't want to feel it.

It's okay to have these questions. It's natural to have these feelings. My family felt them all when they discovered I was gay while I was still in middle school. But as a parent, it's your job to remember that all those questions and feelings come secondary to your primary responsibility: loving your LGBTQ child.

What I didn't realize at that age was how scared and confused my family was as well. They weren't equipped to have this conversation just as much as I wasn't prepared to come out. We had all heard the same abstract messages about my sexuality in our church community, and there were few (if any) resources available to help my family work through the implications of my sexuality in a healthy and loving way. At the end of the day, we all felt alone in our own ways, and the effects of this loneliness created deep wounds in our relationship that would take a decade or more to begin healing.

So what do you do if your child comes out to you?

Brian says,

> The answer is simple: you love them. Yes, you may be over-whelmed by a world of emotions. And it's okay to have them. But in that moment, you simply show them love. You don't need to have the answers. You don't need to have figured out how sexuality and faith may or may not work together. You'll have time to work through those questions together if you handle this one interaction [coming out] with love. In that sacred moment, your child is looking for only one thing: your embrace.
>
> It's okay that you haven't worked through your approach to sexuality. It's okay to feel unprepared as an abstract theology you thought you had suddenly becomes uncomfortably concrete. You may be just as unprepared as my parents were when they discovered my secret. Maybe your reputation at church suffers when this becomes public. Maybe people will talk about you and your child behind your back. None of that matters. If you can continue to love your child through that defining moment, you'll show them that you are someone they can trust as you work together to find the answers you both need.

In a very unscientific poll, I asked my Facebook and Twitter followers to tell me what they'd do if their teen came out to them as LGBTQ. By and large, people responded with "love them unconditionally" and "my love for them never changes." One father said he would "love his child, ask questions, and point to the truth of what the Scriptures say about marriage between a man and wife, knowing that sometimes men aren't attracted to women, and women aren't attracted to men. This does not mean God made a mistake."

Even as I finished this manuscript, a young man who identified as a woman recently committed suicide and made national headlines. A pastor, who wishes to remain anonymous, offers this advice for parents when they find themselves lost in the uncharted territory of sexual orientation and identification:

> Transgender issues are becoming more and more a part of the discussion both inside and outside the church. And as of right now Christians are behind in their efforts to offer a biblically informed and humane response. We need both a deeper understanding of what people are experiencing and of biblical teaching.

But for now, here are some biblical principles that can help a Christian parent respond to their child's deep personal struggle:

1. **Their child isn't a mistake.** According to the Bible, God created all people in his image (Gen. 1:26–27), and we are fearfully and wonderfully made (Ps. 139:14).
2. **God has an unfathomable love for all people (John 3:16).**
3. **This world isn't the way God intended it to be.** When sin infiltrated the world, God's creation became plagued with brokenness and dysfunction (Rom. 8:18–21). Everyone is affected. Like the world, we, too, are not the way we are supposed to be (Gen. 3). Sin has corrupted every part of every person. This means sin has tainted our minds, bodies, relationships, work, feelings, and words. *Every part of us.*
4. **Thankfully, Jesus redeems sinners (Rom. 5:8).** Through the cross on which Jesus died to pay the penalty of humanity's sin, God redeems everything (Col. 1:20), including the world and our lives. He invites everyone to

turn from sin and follow him. The only way to become a Christian is by grace (Eph. 2:8–9).

5. **Jesus understands.** He is not aloof. He is *Immanuel*, which means "God with us." He faces the trials and temptations we face (Heb. 2:17–18).

6. **Following Jesus is essential.** God has planned a unique race for each of us (Heb. 12:2). No two races are the same. That's fine. Every Christian parent hopes their child puts their faith in Jesus, seeing in him God's splendor and glory and desiring more of him (2 Cor. 4:4–6).

7. **God will use this struggle for good.** At this moment it's difficult to believe that such a trial could ever be used for good. But God promises it will. He will use it to keep the struggling parent dependent on him, to humble them, and to create in them a compassion for others. God can and will use this situation to make them more like Jesus (Rom. 8:29).

8. **This is a long, difficult journey, and good friends are important to have.** No one who reads Jesus's words would think becoming a Christian means life will be trouble-free (Acts 14:22). Actually, the Bible notes that we will experience trials beyond our ability to bear alone. That's why God promises to go with us (Isa. 43:1–3). The Bible also emphasizes the importance of having worthy friends who will help one another "to stir up love and good works" (Heb. 10:24).

9. **One day every Christian will be with Jesus, our struggle will end, and we will experience everlasting joy (Rev. 21:1–5).** The apostle Paul anticipated the day when he would depart from this world and forever be in Jesus's

presence. Being with our Savior is far better than any-thing this world has to offer (Phil. 1:21–24), for in God's presence there are "pleasures forevermore" (Ps. 16:11).[17]

▶ THE BOTTOM LINE

If you feel overwhelmed, terrified, scared, hurt, concerned, or confused, *it's okay.* I've been in student ministry in one capacity or another, including as a youth pastor's wife, for the last fifteen years. Every week I connect with students who have questions, who are facing delicate issues, or who tell me something about sex I didn't know before.

Tim and I have spent many days and nights discussing the challenges and consequences students this age face. Some are the same challenges you and I confronted when we were grow-ing up. Some are entirely different. But one thing I've learned is this: *your teenager wants to talk to you but is afraid.* I can't tell you how many times I've had serious discussions with high school girls who have questions about sex and dating. My first response is always, "What does your mom or dad think?" When they reply, as they often do, that they could *never* talk to their parents about sex because they're afraid to, I encourage them to try. But here's my advice to you: Alleviate the fear your child is experiencing. Make the first move. Initiate the conversation, and then keep it going.

The purpose of this chapter is to offer you a framework and some talking points that will help you initiate conversations about sex with your child, no matter their age. Your overall goal is to establish yourself as trustworthy—to communicate to your kids that you are an open book and a safe person with whom to talk about sex. Be honest and don't shame, regardless of your emotional reaction to the conversations. Above all, pray for your child daily as they mature from an infant to a preschooler to a teenager to an adult. Prayer will protect and sustain you and your child like nothing else can.

EXPERTS WANT YOU TO KNOW

Rhett Smith, MDiv, MSMFT, is a licensed marriage and family therapist in private practice in Plano, Texas. He is passionate about helping couples, families, and adolescents transform their relationships and experience a thriving life. Rhett is a graduate of Fuller Theological Seminary and the author of *The Anxious Christian* and *What It Means to be a Man.* He lives in McKinney, Texas, with his wife, Heather, and their two children. You can find out more about Rhett's work and writing at rhettsmith.com.

Parents always want to know the proper time to talk to their children about sex. What general guidelines would you give them?

My general rule of thumb is that you should start much earlier than you think. By the time most parents get around to talking to their kids about sex, if at all, they have been exposed to more pornography and sexuality than their parents were in their first thirty years or more. Often I will have a parent say to me, "My ten-year-old isn't interested in sex or naked women," but the reality is that the average age of exposure to pornography for boys is somewhere between ages five and nine (both research and my own experience with clients support this). You have to initiate the conversation early.

Begin by talking with your young children about their bodies, appropriate and inappropriate touch, strangers and touch, etc.

Also, think of talking to your kids about sex as a lifelong process and not a onetime deal. The era of the "birds and bees" talk is long gone. You need to think about encouraging and being available for conversations with your kids all along the way, and specifically at different developmental milestones. I encourage parents to have talks at important stages like entering school, throughout elementary school, in middle school, junior high, high school, college, and even into adulthood. As you can imagine, your child is different sexually at each of these stages, so a single talk won't suffice. And the more you talk to your kids along the way, the more likely they are to open up to you at each stage.

Last, be consistent. Just keep making yourself available and showing up for talks. And even if your kids refuse to talk to you ninety-nine times, it may be that one hundredth encounter that is amazing. They may tell you all kinds of stuff and ask all kinds of questions. But if you aren't there for the first ninety-nine times, then they won't trust you, and you won't experience that one hundredth time. Parents too often give up, saying, "My kid won't talk to me about sex." That's okay. Keep showing up.

On the same note, one of the greatest fears parents have is talking about sex or pornography too early, thereby inciting curiosities that may not have already

existed. Can you share a little bit about how the brain develops from childhood into adolescence and how proper communication can help guide a child's sexual development both mentally and emotionally?

Let me start by saying this: the research and my clinical experience show that we can never talk to our kids too early about sex and pornography. If we wait too long, someone else is going to teach them. It may be their friend, a website, or a YouTube video all the kids are watching at school. So start early, but know that the conversations will be different. You can talk to your four- and five-year-old about appropriate and inappropriate touch as they begin to understand their bodies. You can talk to your six-, seven-, and eight-year-old about their bodies and boundaries by reminding them to shut doors when they bathe or go to the bathroom. And along the way you are talking to them about your value system and why you believe certain things. And you can imagine that as kids get older, your conversations will get more sophisticated as you begin to talk with them about online pornography and sexuality. And by the time you are talking to your nine- and ten-year-old, you may be talking about how the body works sexually and how you expect them to behave. As kids get older and gain more freedom, the conversations will keep changing. For example, they may have their own computer, start dating, etc. So you'll still be talking, but the topics will shift.

I don't believe a parent will incite a curiosity that isn't already there or for which someone else hasn't already planted the seed. Either the parents are going to take responsibility to teach their kids these things or someone else will without hesitation. And since someone else is going to teach them regardless, isn't it important for parents to at least have a say in the matter? If parents want a say, they can't wait until their child is thirteen or sixteen years old. That conversation has to have begun years back. Trust has to be established over time.

I'm definitely not the brain expert, but I know enough neuroscience to be dangerous. We know the brain is not fully developed until sometime around age twenty-five to twenty-eight. Until the brain is fully developed, what drives most kids' behavior is not the logical part of the brain, which develops later, but the primal fight or flight part. Kids are naturally going to respond with emotions, feelings, and sensations. Sex and pornography are the perfect combination to incite these things in a kid's brain.

This is why it's important for parents to be a part of the conversation and help bring insight and knowledge to their child's understanding of sexuality. Otherwise, when there is a lack of communication in this area, a child will often default to what feels good.

What things do parents do that discourage a child from forming a healthy view of sexuality?

A parent's silence discourages a child from forming a healthy view of sexuality. Silence communicates so many things, but around the issue of sexuality it often communicates judgment, shame, and perversion. When parents are silent on the matter, kids will find something to fill that silence. And often what fills the void for kids is the discovery of unhealthy and destructive behaviors around sex.

Parents also discourage a child from forming a healthy view of sexuality by failing to make an open and safe environment in which they can talk about difficult topics. If their surrounding environment isn't open and safe, kids aren't going to want to talk and engage with parents, which will lead them to seek out an environment that feels safe to them. Very often kids feel safe online because they can look at a screen and not be judged. They can be in control.

Parents also often make offhand comments about sexuality. Kids pick up on this and form their own judgments. So be careful what you say around your kids because they are listening to you and observing and noting your attitude about sex.

Lastly, and it's been mentioned already, but shaming is huge. Shame is when a person thinks, *I've done something or seen something or thought something, and therefore I'm bad. Something is wrong with me.* And when someone internalizes their shame, it causes them to cut off communication and connection.

Many kids are just curious. They have questions about the human body, or they were attracted to a naked picture on a screen. And rather than parents talking about it with them and helping them explore their curiosity and creating an opportunity for a deeper connection, parents take the quick and easy way out. They shame their kids and hope that will keep them from repeating the behavior or asking questions that make them uncomfortable.

Instead, let your kids know it's natural to be curious about sexuality, and talk to them about it. Use that curiosity to reframe the discussion around sex, emphasizing that it is a beautiful thing that God has created. Remind them that God has a purpose for sex, which is why we need to set healthy boundaries concerning it. Help kids understand the connection between the beauty of sex and the values you hold as parents and as a family.

What are the best things parents can do to help a child form a healthy view of sexuality?

In addition to fostering an ongoing, open conversation about sexuality, parents can use real-life opportunities to engage in conversations about sexuality, rather than feeling required to deliver a serious talk. For example, if you see something on TV that is sexually unhealthy and not in line with your values, rather than simply changing the station and ignoring it, talk about why it doesn't align with your family's beliefs. Tell your kids what you believe and why it's important. Or if you see one of their friends treating another person in a sexually inappropriate way, take time to talk about why that behavior's not right and what you want for your child.

Your kids will likely forget a onetime talk or be too embarrassed to really listen to you. Instead, use everyday teaching moments to engage in conversation. Those individual conversations will add up to a much more powerful and healthier sexual ethic for your child.

2

Your Child Is Not the Exception

The Ineffectiveness of Sheltering and What to Do Instead

"The thing is that most parents think their kid is the exception."

Those were a pastor's words to me after I'd reported to him that two students had confessed abuse to me. A young woman had shared (for the first time) that she had been sexually abused, and another young man admitted that a family member had shown him pornography during the time they spent together. I am a mandatory reporter (someone who has to report suspected abuse to Child Protective Services or to local law enforcement), but since these were the pastor's students (and he was also a mandatory reporter), I wanted him to be the first point of contact.

"What do you mean parents think their child is the exception?" I asked the pastor.

"If you look around, you'll notice most of the kids that came to this youth camp are our standard churchgoing kids," he responded. "They don't fall on the fringes. Most people assume things like incest or promiscuity only happen to the kids on the outside of a church community. Even when we tell them, which we will, it's going to be difficult for parents to accept some of the things we heard this week."

Sure enough, that's exactly what happened. When the youth staff members returned to their home church and gave the parents a report of what had happened over the week—keeping the public report general—some parents were appreciative, but most were angry that the church condoned talking about sexuality. Many were also in denial that their children already had been exposed to what our culture says about sex. Their responses lend themselves to a question we'll address a little later in this chapter: We know our role as parents, and we know what the media is telling our kids, but does the church also have a role in talking about sex?

A few weeks later, I spoke at a church in a small coastal vacation town where second homes, big boats, nice restaurants, and churches on every block are the norm. After my talk, a grandfather of a six-year-old asked to have his book signed and proceeded to tell me he had just learned that his son, the six-year-old's father, was selling nude photos of the child and exploiting him sexually to obtain money for alcohol.

"It really can happen to anyone, anywhere," he said, grief scrawled all over his face.

The reality is that nobody—child or adult—is an exception. We will *all* face temptation, and as the Scriptures say, we pretty much face the same temptations. In 1 Corinthians 10:13, Paul writes, "*The temptations in your life are no different from what others experience. And God is faithful. He will not allow the temptation to be more than you can stand. When you are tempted, he will show you a way out so that you can endure*" (NLT, emphasis added). The question is, will the way out be through you, the parent? Will you give your children the knowledge and wisdom to respond to abusive situations or sexual temptation?

Earlier this year I met an elementary school teacher who learned some of her students had used their mobile phones to take pictures of themselves in various stages of undress. They'd sent the pictures to other classmates with cell phones, who then showed the pictures to children without phones.

Thinking that eight- and nine-year-olds seemed awfully young to have phones (and to use them in such a manner), I consulted a reliable source: my mom.

My mom has been an elementary school teacher in one of the more disadvantaged school districts in the Dallas area for more than twenty years. Almost all the children she teaches receive free lunches and other government assistance. I assumed, based on simple socioeconomics, that fewer, if any, of her students would have cell phones compared to the national average. Turns out, I was wrong.

"Oh, definitely. I would say a majority of our third and fourth graders have cell phones," she assured me.

"Even in your school?" I asked, just to clarify. "Are they smartphones?"

"Yes. Every kid who has a phone has a smartphone. I'm the only one with a dumb phone in the third-grade hall."

Even if your child doesn't have a mobile phone, they know someone who does. Kids have access to far more technology than we might assume.

After I published the post "Three Things You Don't Know about Your Kids and Sex" on my blog, people responded with comments equal parts grateful, angry, and in denial. Yet what happened a month after the post went live was telling.

Here is one of the replies I received:

> I read your post about a month ago, and at that time I was praying my child would be the exception. But I found her using YouTube to watch "kissing" videos. I am heartbroken and in tears. We are a strong Christian family. I feel a load on my shoulders like never before. She is only ten.

And this:

> I appreciate your story, but I was certain there was no way my seven-year-old knew about pornography. He has his own iPad for games and limited internet. My iPad broke, and when I borrowed his, I was shocked to see hardcore gay pornography on it. It wasn't just one page either. I could tell he was searching for certain words. I asked him the next day if he knew what those words meant, and he didn't. He heard them at school and looked them up. I thought we did everything to protect our child, but I am at a complete loss.

This message was from a teenage girl:

> This was interesting to read, especially as a teenage girl who has struggled with this. I thought I was the exception. For

quite a while in my life, I thought I was the screwed up Christian girl.

From my own experience, everything you have said was true. I looked up words that I had no idea what they meant. I was too ashamed to ask my parents about them because people acted like they were such dirty words that I thought I couldn't ask.

And this from another teenage girl:

I am a seventeen-year-old Christian girl who accepted the Lord as my Savior when I was four. I fully love the Lord. When I was nine years old, I started looking things up on Google about sex, and it just went from there, like you said. I watched porn until I was fifteen years old and even started masturbating. I have confessed my sin, and the Lord has forgiven me, but forgiving myself is a struggle. And I still deal with the temptation to fall back into my old sinful nature in this area. I haven't told anyone about this, but I wish parents and adults could know and understand that kids are interested, and they know so much more than you think! The internet is a terrible trap, and the devil finds his way.

This message from a mother who was trying her best to raise a godly family shows how many different ways kids can be reached:

My husband and I thought our kids were the exception because we have been very careful with their exposure to TV, movies, internet, friends, etc. However, we recently discovered that our thirteen-year-old son was texting with girls from around the world and getting very graphic pictures on his phone! We are the exact kind of family you describe . . . I am a Vacation Bible School leader and a preschool churchtime teacher, and my husband is a deacon and teaches our couples' Sunday school class. Our children have been very involved in church all their lives, but it still happened to us. It can happen to anyone![1]

Sheltering Is Not the Answer

In the fall of 2014, Kim Kardashian's nude photos went viral on social media, and once they did, it was almost impossible to avoid them. I know, because I stumbled on the photos myself without even looking as I was scrolling through Instagram, a social media photo sharing site.

After browsing my friend's images, I clicked the "Explore" tab (which normally shows me photos my friends have liked, as well as the most popular photos on Instagram), and within moments of the page loading, I was exposed to every new Photoshopped picture of Kim's naked body (and several crude memes mocking it). Even though these photos violated Instagram's terms of service, they became the most popular photos on the social network and were seen by millions of people before Instagram could take them down. After they removed the first wave of Kardashian's photos, the pictures kept getting reposted and repopularized. It was impossible for me to avoid seeing them (unless I avoided Instagram for the next several days, which is what I did).

My friend Annie Downs is an author and speaker who writes for teen girls and adults. When she saw what was happening with the Kardashian photos, Annie addressed the situation immediately on her blog and social media channels.

If you haven't seen, new nude magazine cover photos were released of Kim Kardashian this week (it's not the first time, but it surely seems to be the most viral release). . . . It has been hard, nearly impossible, to avoid seeing her full backside displayed, and as of yesterday, her full front side as well. And while I hope you can get around the internet without passing by these images, most won't be able to. If you can avoid seeing them, do. If you can protect your children from seeing the photos, do.

Instead of reinventing the wheel and writing my own response, I shared Annie's article with those who follow me online. Most people who follow me know that sexuality and pornography are topics I frequently discuss.

Annie's blog post garnered more than two million views that day. Predictably, a conversation ensued across the many channels where it was posted. For the most part, parents and girls were thankful for her quick, gracious, no-nonsense response. But some were indignant and offended:

"What kind of world do we live in that our elementary school–age kids even know who Kim Kardashian is? My children sure don't!"

They weren't only appalled that Kim Kardashian "broke the internet" (as Kim later referred to the campaign), they were offended and surprised that Annie, a faith-based author, had addressed the topic at all. Many of the parents who responded assumed the topic was neither relevant nor a threat to their children and responded with things like:

"This is why my kids are homeschooled" (or "in private school").

"This is why we don't allow our children to use technology!"

"Our school's library has a filter on it—there's no way they saw it!"

While it makes me incredibly sad that we live in a world in which children are exposed to explicit images they should never see, the reality is that *we do live in that world.* We live in a society where two-year-olds have iPads. Most children *will* stumble on pornography.

Homeschooling may offer slightly more protection against your child's exposure to objectionable material, but it's not a guarantee. At some point, your child will be in a situation in which they will be confronted with explicit images, words, or ideas. You can implement every filter and monitoring program I suggest in the resource section of this book. You can limit Wi-Fi. You can monitor your child's internet use and keep the closest eye on your family as humanly possible. You can run all the background checks on babysitters and make sure you don't live near registered sex offenders.

You can be careful.

You can be wise.

But you cannot ever be in complete control.

This is why trying to shelter your child from explicit sexual material is not a viable solution. However, communicating with them is.

My friend Adam McClane has worked in youth ministry for more than twenty years. I love what he told me about sheltering versus communicating:

> I don't like to use terms such as sheltered or safe. I prefer to talk to teenagers (and parents) about health. A parent shouldn't, and ultimately can't, aim to keep their child safe. (Many aim to do exactly that, but no one is completely successful; that's simply a fallacy.) This is particularly true for Christian parents as we recognize that a life following Jesus isn't meant to be a calling toward safety. Instead, we should

aim for health and wholeness in Christ. If, as a parent, I process things through the lens of this question—"What do I need to do to help my child be healthy?"—I can see that it's not healthy to set up prohibitions. Instead, it's healthy to talk about what God wants for us . . . healthy relationships, a healthy mind, and sexual health. Talking about healthy sexuality goes beyond the mechanics and focuses on the emotional connection developed between two people in the act of sex.

The "Really Good Christian" Family

I recently met a children's minister at a church I visited. As we were making small talk, she casually asked me if I was writing a new book.

I love this question.

When I tell someone I'm writing a book about opening up the conversation between parents and children about sex, I'm usually met with one of two responses: deer-in-the-headlights horror or extreme excitement. In this case, she was *ecstatic*.

"OH. MY. GOODNESS. That book is SO needed today. Can I read it now? Can I order it somewhere? When does it come out? People think the church is exempt from this or that it only happens to teenage boys," she explained. "At our Vacation Bible School, I walked into the ladies room and heard what ended up being a second grader masturbating in a stall. Now, I'm pretty open about sex, but I was shocked. It was clear she wasn't just exploring herself, either. She was doing it for sexual gratification. After I talked to her about it, I learned she had a history of sexual abuse. Nobody's exempt from this. Parents, pastors, and even leaders in children's and student ministry need to know how to handle situations like this with grace and love and hope."

Her words *nobody's exempt* reminded me of what the first youth pastor said: everyone thinks their child is the exception. It's simply not true, even in "good Christian" homes. During my most innocent days, I wasn't the exception. In junior high, there was a cute boy my age who lived close to the church my father pastored. After discovering the chemistry (read: hormones) between us, we snuck out of Sunday school early and went behind the church to make out.

It was awkward, and I remember thinking how his sparse facial hair scratched my face. We weren't behind the church for more than two minutes when a deacon in the church (who stepped out for a smoke) found us. It's now a family joke at holidays, but in the moment, my parents were *livid*. Here I was, the new preacher's kid, sneaking out of Sunday school to kiss a boy.

My husband and I know a terrific couple. The father has a well-respected career and a postgraduate degree, and the mother is a stay-at-home mom. They are involved with their church and community and are kind, generous, and wise. They have three children: thirteen- and twelve-year-old boys and an eight-year-old girl. Their eldest son has Asperger's syndrome (a disorder on the autism spectrum).

In their community, most churchgoing families keep the subject of sex hush-hush. Yet in an email to me, the mother explained how even in the most hands-on and aware families, these conversations are important, as well as challenging and sometimes unexpected:

> We've hit this head-on in our home in the last eighteen months. We had individual "birds and bees" (what a lame label for that conversation!) talks with our boys using a Dobson-ish book about three years ago. Ray [the younger

son], with his tirelessly scientific, questioning mind, was curious about the topic without much testosterone behind it. It only took one unprotected iPad at our house to change that.

A few innocent searches quickly led him down an ugly path. He gets it now. He understands those feelings are normal, and he is not ashamed. He talks to us regularly about it, but he still squirms if we say the word *porn*. He asked if I would refer to it as *popcorn*. Kids are funny.

Paul's story was a little tougher. Mixing full-on puberty with Asperger's syndrome has made for some sleepless nights. We had the same talk with prepubescent Paul, and he couldn't have cared less about it. About six months later, some kid at school showed him how easy it was to get past the school internet filter and introduced him to some really disgusting porn.

The heart of most of Paul's social issues lie in his inability to discern appropriate from inappropriate and make sense of the overwhelming flood of sensory information his brain perceives. Applying this to the images he saw made for a very confused kid. He had a hard time telling what was somewhat normal and what was truly obscene and even deviant, but those images sure were enticing, whatever they were! It has taken lots of graphic gloves-off conversations to help him conceptualize what is normal and what is not. Things just take longer with Paul, whether we're talking about tying shoes or phone greetings or making friends or character development. He frequently says to his dad, "Dad, just make sure Ray doesn't get into this stuff." I love him.

His dad and I have gone to really great lengths to be sure he has no access to pornography at home, and I think the distance from it has allowed him to "sober up" a little and gain some perspective.

I was delighted to hear about how this family has approached the topic of sex and pornography with their children, especially understanding the way their son Paul interprets these things. They know the reality of what their kids face, even as a great, churchgoing, God-fearing family, and they aren't afraid to talk about it . . . continually. They set a great example from which we can all learn.

Sometimes, even the most proactive parents face challenges. My friend Michelle introduced me to Jen Sandbulte, who recently posted an article on her blog about discovering pornography on her daughter's iPod.

Jen writes:

> If it can happen at my house, it can happen anywhere. I don't say that because I am proud; quite the opposite.
>
> I am passionate about human trafficking, and because of this passion, I spend a good deal of time talking about the dangers of pornography and how it feeds the demand for human trafficking. To say that we are a house that has buried our head in the sand and just ignored the issues is absolutely *not* the truth. We haven't looked the other way.
>
> I have spent a great deal of time talking to our boys about pornography. Not because they are boys, but because they are older. Our daughter Emma is eight, and we have talked about it some, but not to the degree my boys and I have. All our devices have safety features set, and all our YouTube apps also have safety set to on. The kids aren't allowed to take devices into their rooms or into private places. I "thought" we were protected.
>
> You can imagine my surprise when I discovered inappropriate sites on my daughter's iPod. On three different occasions, she was able to access inappropriate material. I was mortified! How had this happened? My heart broke

for my little girl and for what her innocent eight-year-old eyes had seen.

As I was tucking my daughter in and began to talk to her about this, I could instantly see the shame come over her. The look in her eyes is not one I will forget anytime soon. You see, even at the age of eight, the enemy knew how to use his shame to keep her captive instead of to empower her to ask me for help. I switched off my anger and disappointment at her and myself, and instead focused on how Jesus would handle this situation. I called out the shame I saw in her, and she immediately began to get teary eyed. Then we talked about the love of Jesus and the gift of forgiveness. And we prayed. We asked for forgiveness, and we prayed that he would erase those images from her mind and restore her mind back to purity.

Since that first night, we have had some hard talks. I have shared with her that the people and the things she saw were actors and that wasn't how it *really* was. I also explained that some of them may not have been getting treated fairly or paid for what they were forced to do. I was able to do this in an age-appropriate manner but was still undone by having to have these talks with my eight-year-old.

We must be willing to have the hard conversations and to continue to have the hard conversations. We have to continue to check and follow up, to hold accountable and to extend grace.[2]

What Role Does the Church Play?

I once chased a boy through the church and, in my clumsiness, sprained my ankle in the pursuit. While my mother iced my sore ankle in the church's kitchen, the wives of several prominent members and deacons stood by the door and declared that my injury was a result of God's punishment: I shouldn't have been chasing a boy in the church.

Sure, I thought he was cute. That's why I chased him. And he likely felt the same way about me, which is why he played along with me. Instead of dismissing the incident for what it was—an innocent and silly crush—I was left with the understanding that something I naturally felt (a slight attraction to a boy) was frowned upon by God . . . so much so that he would cause me physical harm.

As I mentioned earlier, I grew up attending conferences that preached the importance of virginity as a close second to the importance of salvation. No one ever addressed the grey areas I questioned as a teenager. Questions like, "How far is too far?" and "What *is* masturbation anyway?" The message was clear: as long as I did not have sex, I was okay. The church made virginity into a god, but nothing else—none of the grey areas—was ever discussed.

Naturally, when sexuality is defined in such black-and-white extremes, the likely conclusion—at least from an adolescent's perspective—is that the grey area is free to explore. If the church didn't specifically say it's wrong, then surely it's not a sin, right?

As a good Bible-learning kid does, I eventually flipped through Song of Solomon with my purity ring on my finger and shuddered at the super-sexual descriptions. I couldn't figure out why the church frowned upon sex and *never* talked about it in the way the Bible actually described it.

In my later teenage years, after the sexual abuse and throughout the five-year span when I looked at pornography, I wondered if I should even bother to figure out the grey areas. As long as I chose to say no to sex when I was single, that was all that mattered, right? Deep down in my heart, though, I knew that wasn't the truth. I felt guilty after being physically intimate with someone, even when we didn't have sexual intercourse (commonly referred to as "everything but" [sex]).

I never heard sex talked about in church (except when it was mentioned as sin) until my midtwenties. And when the pastor addressed pornography then, he never said it could be a problem for women too. Porn was a man's problem. I appreciated his candor, but at that point, I was already a couple years removed from my own habits and knew women who shared the same struggles I did.

God eventually led me to share my story and help others in the process. Even now I can't tell you how strange it feels to do what I do for a career. Yet at the same time, one of my favorite things is to talk about sex at church. It sounds kind of strange, I know. But honestly, it brings a little bit of holy satisfaction to my spirit to speak light and truth about a topic the church has largely avoided—or talked shamefully about—for most of its recent history. Thankfully, many churches are beginning to embrace the battle all of us—men, women, *and* children—fight. Leadership is stepping up and addressing our dysfunctions while offering help to those who need it. It's no longer as taboo as it once was to talk about sex.

When I do speak at churches about sex, pornography, and abuse—both to parents and students—I get a lot of mixed feedback. Many parents are grateful that I opened the proverbial can of worms. Sometimes, if a church didn't communicate well with parents or with the church body beforehand, my message can be a little shocking. One woman pulled me aside after I shared my story during a Sunday morning worship service and blurted out, "My eleven-year-old asked me what pornography was after you said it."

I couldn't read her countenance well. Was she upset? Thankful? I chose the safe route and apologized.

"No," she responded. "I *needed* to have this conversation. I just wish I had been the first person he heard it from. But thank you for pushing me to have it now."

I couldn't agree more with her sentiment. *The church should not be the first responder in the conversation about sex.* Although more and more churches are talking about healthy, biblical sexuality, this doesn't dismiss parents from starting and continuing that conversation. At most, the church should be a partner to walk alongside you and your family as you navigate these largely uncharted waters.

But the church isn't off the hook either. If your church avoids weighty topics like sexuality, pornography, or abuse education, it's up to you to insist they address it. Talk to other parents and members of your church. Meet with the leadership. Suggest a forum. Research potential speakers, experts, and counselors who can contribute to the conversation. Talk about it in your small groups or Sunday school classes. I'm happy to come out and talk with you about it too.

My favorite events are the ones where a church boldly embraces honest, biblical conversation about sexuality. At one such event, the church invited both parents and students to attend. The parents sat on the floor level of the auditorium and the students, ages twelve to eighteen, sat in the balcony. I spoke with the pastor before the event to ensure we were on the same page. One of the things I've learned as a speaker is that in some situations, words like *pornography* or *masturbation* distract more than teach, and I want to respect each church's specific culture.

Before introducing me, the pastor thanked both the parents and the students for attending the event, acknowledging that it was brave of them. The church leadership, he explained, had realized the importance of addressing topics like sexual abuse, pornography, masturbation, oral sex, anal sex . . . he continued with a laundry list of sexual topics that were relevant to the event. I was surprised but appreciative.

I'm sure most of the people who attended that event were startled as well and heard a little more than they had bargained for, but the church had prepared well. Prior to the event, they had equipped parents with resources and statistics. They invited me to share my story of hope and freedom and then followed up with even more resources and well-trained volunteers.

The "shock-and-awe" approach isn't right for everyone, but I do think too often we make the mistake of playing it safe out of fear. We worry we'll offend and alienate, when, instead, we should bravely speak up about the gift of sex. The enemy is trying to destroy this gift from God. We need to set the story straight.

Author and pastor Erwin McManus once said that culture listens to those who tell the best story. Is the church telling the best (and most accurate) story about sex? Or are the quiet narratives the church shares drowned out by the cacophony of our culture and the media? We *have* to speak up and share the real story of sex. And we need to ask the church to begin to share the responsibility with us.

▶ THE BOTTOM LINE

Your child is not the exception.

The reality is that you cannot shelter your child from the world. *Someone* is going to tell your child about sex and pornography. Someone is going to define what "sexy" is. Your child will hear words you don't want them to hear and potentially see things you don't want them to see. And the hard truth is that you have little control over this.

What you *can* control is the conversation, as well as from whom your child first learns about sex.

How do you want your child to learn about sex? From a peer? The media? A photo of a scantily dressed model hanging in the window of a lingerie store at the mall? If you want them to learn the values you have established in your home, you need to have this conversation. Don't be afraid that it will spark unnecessary curiosity. It might, but because you are being proactive, you can help guide what happens next.

EXPERTS WANT YOU TO KNOW

Jen Sandbulte is a mother, wife, human resources professional, and passionate advocate for survivors of human trafficking. She is currently president of J.S. Leadership Group, is a certified Senior Professional in Human Resources, and holds an MBA from the University of South Dakota. She is also president and founder of Simply Grace Ministries and founder and manager of the annual COMPEL Conference for women. Jen leads weekly prayer meetings to combat human trafficking and has attended multiple training programs on both pornography and human trafficking. Jen and her husband, Tom, live in Iowa, where they are active parents of three young children and two adult children.

Why do some parents think their child will be the exception to being exposed to a sexually inundated culture?

I think as parents we tend to assume we have done everything to protect our kids and have taught them to make appropriate choices. In our case (when our eight-year-old daughter was exposed to online pornography), we had the controls—filters, software, family rules, etc.—in place. While we had spoken frequently about the dangers of pornography to our twin boys, we never expected that our younger daughter would be the one exposed to it so early.

I know what the statistics cite as the common age for first exposure, and I started talking to my twin boys well before they reached that age. I assumed my daughter was still "safe"—she is only eight—so I hadn't had as many conversations with her yet about the dangers of pornography. I had the YouTube safety on and the proper settings on her iPod checked, but inappropriate images still made it in front of her eyes.

My husband and I are the couple that "should" have kids who know better, and a house that "should" be protected from accidental exposure. I am involved with campaigning against human trafficking, and because of past incidents and hurts, I have talked openly with all my kids about their bodies, their private parts, sexuality, everything. My husband is also actively involved in campaigning against human trafficking and knows that pornography use spurs the desire for increased pornography use. I guess we assumed we were covered, that we'd done everything possible to protect our kids. But discovering porn on my daughter's iPod made me realize that simply wasn't the case.

Is it possible for children to be too protected or too sheltered? And if so, what implications might this have in the long run?

I think it is possible. I'm always a bit concerned when I see that, because we can only control so much. As I look at the research, it's clear that compulsive pornography use spans all social and economic classes, races, and religious backgrounds—clearly no one is entirely protected from exposure. Yet, as parents, it's natural to assume that we can do enough to make sure our kids are safe. While there *are* several things we can do to *help* keep them safe, including, first and foremost, purposeful prayer—praying that God protects their eyes and their desires—none of these measures is entirely fail-safe.

I know parents who have eliminated internet access in their homes and have chosen to homeschool their children to decrease the negative impact of other kids. But even these comparatively dramatic measures aren't foolproof. And they certainly don't take the place of education and open conversation with our kids about biblical sexuality and the dangers of pornography. Are these hard, awkward conversations? Yes, absolutely! But hard and awkward is better than the alternative, which is that your kids explore pornography without your knowledge and perhaps fall deeper and deeper into a dangerous cycle. It's imperative that we create an open, comfortable environment that allows our kids to ask questions and talk to us about anything *without condemnation.*

Whether your kids are eight, eighteen, or twenty-eight, the point will come when they will leave your home and have access to technology. In essence, they will be responsible for making their own choices. At some point they will need to be aware enough to avoid pornography, yet at the same time know they can talk to you about it if they are struggling. Ongoing prayer and open conversation (using age-appropriate terminology and details that help them understand why pornography is harmful) are the most effective strategies for helping to keep our children safe.

Can we keep our kids safe? How (or why not)?

Many parents won't like to hear this, but I'm not 100 percent convinced we can keep our kids from seeing pornography at some point. I am certainly an advocate for putting controls in place. However, I'm also a huge advocate for prayer, conversation, and realistic advice.

For example, as we continue to talk openly about pornography with our boys, both Tom and I are real with them. Say, for instance, our boys are at a friend's house and someone accesses pornography. We talk about how our first choice would be for them to stand up to their friends and be a leader, but we also tell them we understand that taking this kind of initiative is very, very hard, especially in the face of peer pressure. So we've also suggested some practical ideas. For example, the "escape plan" is where they can excuse themselves to the restroom, which would give them a quick out and time to think. They can call us or pray about what to say when they go back into the room or decide when they return that they are going to hang out in a different part of the room. I don't want to offer my kids only one solution, the "right" solution. As parents, we have to be realistic about the realities of peer pressure. At the same time, I also don't want to give them permission to join in just because it's hard to say no. It's a fine line.

In my daughter's situation, a classmate had told her to check out a few particular websites, and she did. She wasn't on the sites for long, but it's still been a struggle to erase those images from her young eight-year-old mind. Honestly, the situation could have been a lot worse and might still be going on if we hadn't talked with our kids about pornography in the first place or encouraged them to come to us with their questions.

3

Kids Consume Sexual Messages through Mainstream Media

A Quick Review of What's Out There and How to Address It

People in our developed, westernized, high-tech culture are inundated by thousands of media messages a day. Television, radio, logos, packaging, billboards, internet ads, email lists, snail mail, bumper stickers, movies—whether it's overt or obscure, the ways media influences our lives are endless. Allow me to perform a real-time unscientific experiment. It's 1:03 p.m. on a Saturday afternoon in December. I'm sitting in an independent coffeehouse, mostly frequented by graduate students from the local state university and the occasional coffee snob (like me). Imagine you're sitting nearby. Now we're going to take a 360-degree glance around the inside of the café and note any sort of media or message displayed in the café itself or attached to any patron (anything that is at least popular enough to recognize).

From left to right, here we go:

- The "Texas Star" emblem
- Oak Cliff Coffee Roasters (a well-known Texas coffee roaster)
- Three Apple laptops
- Dell laptop
- Three iPhones
- CamelBak water container
- Victoria's Secret "Love Pink" brand laptop sleeve (side note: Victoria's Secret makes laptop sleeves?)
- Nike sweatshirt
- North Face backpack
- Bose headphones
- A man wearing a shirt with various sponsors on it, including Schlotzsky's, Allstate, United Supermarkets, Planet Fitness, and a handful of others that are hidden by his Columbia jacket, which is thrown over the back of his chair
- The streaming radio station currently playing a Carrie Underwood song followed by an ad for MasterCard offering a chance to meet Gwen Stefani (wait, is this 1996 again?)
- My husband texted me a link to a site that compared dogs to their famous literary owners.* On it, I saw an

*It's hilarious. Here's a link to the original site without ads: http://www.dan bannino.com/portfolio/poetic-dogs/.

ad for a story about a girl who went from "frumpy" to "sexy" and is now getting revenge on her ex-lovers.

Compiling that quick list took about thirty seconds, and the messages and products I "consumed" are relatively harmless. However, if I were sitting in your average restaurant or bar, strolling through a mall, driving from this coffeehouse to my home, or even just browsing the internet, I know the messages would be more risqué and sexualized. I know the liquor or clothing ads on TV, the lingerie stores and life-size posters of models I'd pass in the mall. I've seen the sexy billboards for beer products and the advertisements for strip clubs while driving on the interstate. Even on respected news websites, I know the suggested (and suggestive) articles and ads that would come my way.

Our eyes take in whatever is in front of us. If we're emotionally and spiritually developed and healthy, we know how to process that information. If an attractive woman walks by, I can notice her beauty but not compare myself to her. I can choose to listen to my own music instead of the popular radio station in the coffee shop that plays songs that are, at times, inappropriate.

However, if we're not psychologically developed and spiritually mature—which children and most teenagers are not—we don't always know how to process things. Not every message is bad, but we need to learn how to discern and react to what the media feeds us, because the truth is that unless we live completely unplugged from society, we're going to be inundated by the messages companies and advertisers want us to see, hear, and experience. And like the food we eat, the messages we consume will affect our bodies and our brains.

115

This statement by author James P. Steyer perfectly sums up our media-saturated world:

> Unlike the children of the 1950s, 1960s, and 1970s, whose media choices were limited and stood out like isolated, familiar landmarks in communal life, kids today inhabit an environment saturated and shaped by a complex "mediascape" that envelops and bombards them day and night.[1]

All eighteen studies I researched on the influence of mainstream media concluded that the more a child or teen (between all studies, aged seven to seventeen) consumed media with sexual content (sexual images, language, or story lines), their risk of "early sexual intercourse" increased dramatically, especially around the age of fourteen. At that age, those who had a "high sexual media diet" (high SMD) were two times more likely to have sex than their "low sexual media diet" (low SMD) counterparts. And at the age of sixteen? Those with a high SMD were five times more likely to have sex than their low SMD counterparts. Those in the middle were three and a half times more at risk than those who consumed less sexual media.[2]

One expert summed up the research well: "Taken together, the correlation, experimental, and longitudinal studies all speak to the power of the media to educate children and teens about sex and sexuality and to influence their attitudes, beliefs, and behaviors in a significant way."[3]

However, when parents are involved in their children's media consumption, either by coviewing (watching a TV show or movie with the child) or by having a "strong connection" to their children, research indicates that the level of parental involvement actually serves to protect children and teens from the influence of sexual media *and* decreases their likelihood of engaging in sexual intercourse early.

The Moral of the Story

In 2013, I spoke at a convocation at Gordon College in Wenham, Massachusetts. In my talk, I compared watching a TV show in 1988 (when I was eight years old) to watching TV now. I used the popular show *Full House* (which ran from 1987–1995) as an example to illustrate how most television shows portrayed the "moral of the story." Generally, a thirty-minute Friday night program followed this structure:

- Show begins, characters introduced.
- The conflict is presented (i.e., would D.J. go to the party where there would be drinking?).
- The decision is made (she chooses to go).
- The reveal is posed (her father, Danny, finds out and comes to the party to get her, embarrassing her).
- The moral of the story is stated (the conversation between D.J. and Danny explaining the good and bad choices).
- The resolution is played out (D.J. and Danny hug it out).

On almost every show geared toward teenagers at that time, the final five minutes presented the people sitting down, with thoughtful music playing quietly in the background, to discuss the conflict. Why did D.J. want to go to the party? Why didn't she talk to her dad about it first? After the conversation,

D.J. accepted the consequences of her poor choice and understood she could always talk to her dad about peer pressure and ask for his advice, and the scene faded out with a hug between father and daughter.

To contrast my *Full House* story, I paraphrased the plot summary of a current show aimed at a similar demographic that airs on Friday nights: "This guy hooked up with so and so, and she was angry because this other person had also hooked up with someone else. So she decided to hook up with another person to make him jealous."

"The problem," I explained to the Gordon College audience, "is that we've lost the moral of the story. In fact, we've lost the story altogether."

A true story includes character development, conflict, and a resolution. Some, though not all, TV shows (or movies or video games) for children and young adults used to follow a similar story line where the audience would learn something positive at the end. Today, most of our current media content presents only conflict, no story. Because at the end of the day, sex—not story—sells.

In hindsight, even though TV in the '80s was mild compared to programming today, I recently rewatched the first few episodes of *Full House*.* I looked at it through the lens of "What messages am I *really* consuming by watching this?" and was surprisingly disappointed. The show's heartthrob, Uncle Jesse, played by John Stamos, was clearly *very* promiscuous. It's a wonder he didn't father six children and have a plethora of sexually transmitted diseases.†

*Confession: I may or may not own the entire series of *Full House* on DVD.
†I'll be honest. A little part of my childhood died when I realized how much Uncle Jesse slept around.

118

As we'll learn later, sex as it's depicted in mainstream media, including on a "wholesome" show like *Full House*, is rarely connected to physical or emotional consequences.

Children and Media: The Statistics

I recently acquired a textbook, the entirety of which focuses on research relating to children and the media, for a child psychology class.[4] The book literally weighs more than my friend's rat terrier. I spent entire months immersed in it, taking notes on what I should include in this chapter.

The answer? Everything.

From advertising to mainstream media, the internet to video games, this book offers a wealth of data on how children interact with and are affected by various forms of media.

As much as I want to share all the research in this book with you, I can't. First, there's a law against plagiarism. And second, I have only a few pages of this chapter to dedicate to children and the media, and I've likely already spent too many words reminiscing about *Full House*. So let's dig in to some of the most important and relevant statistics as we determine the kinds of media our children consume and how they digest it.

Television

A three-year-old, a nine-year-old, and a fifteen-year-old have a broad and diverse range of interests, and that range is consistent with what children and teens watch on television. A Nielsen study conducted in 2010–2011 revealed that children under the age of twelve watch cartoons and animated features rooted in fantasy. Teens older than thirteen prefer reality shows and sitcoms that reflect their daily lives and experiences.[5]

119

Research indicates that although children and teens watch less TV than adults, on average, they're watching twenty-four hours—a full day of TV—per week. According to one of the most well-respected studies on sex and television, more than 75 percent of prime-time shows on major networks contain sexual content, with only 14 percent portraying any risks or consequences tied to that behavior. The study determined that an average teenager watching average television an average amount of time will be exposed to eight to ten sexual references or behaviors per hour. That's between 192 and 240 exposures to sex per week, just via television. And that study was conducted in 2005, more than ten years ago. Research in media is expensive, and one of the most reputable media research organizations, the Kaiser Family Foundation, closed its media and health section in 2010, so we don't have a truly accurate picture of the current statistics.[6]

In order to conduct my own unscientific experiment, I went to a reliable source to find out what teens watch: the Teen Choice Awards, which airs on Fox each summer. The awards recognize performers in music, television, movies, video games, and internet media, and the winners are chosen by teens. Voters must be between the ages of thirteen and nineteen and live in the United States.

I decided to watch the television show that won the most awards, *Pretty Little Liars* (which airs on ABC Family, a network presently owned by Disney, which, in name alone, implies "family-friendly" programming[7]), and I noted each time something sexual was said, depicted, or implied.

Here's what I observed before the title credits rolled at six minutes in:

Teenagers drinking alcohol, using drugs, and implying that drinking together equates friendship; a tongue-in-cheek comment about one girl being gay; a high school–age girl visiting a pub, where she pretends to be older and flirts with a twenty-three-year-old teacher (they are later shown making out in the pub's bathroom); and a father asking his teenage daughter to keep his affair a secret from her mother.

If you give the show another five minutes, you'll see a teenager flirting with a salesman for $350 sunglasses (which she steals), a teenager offering another teen advice on what clothes to wear and mentioning that she needs to dress sexier to get attention, a flashback scene to the teenage girl accidentally finding her father cheating on her mother, girls wearing really short skirts, and two girls who lost a lot of weight over the summer being called the new, sexy "it" girls. You'll also learn that the teacher who was kissing the high school girl in the pub's bathroom is actually *her* new teacher.

In forty-four minutes, *Pretty Little Liars* contained nearly forty instances of sexual innuendo, content, or language, and many of these references were overt. I watched a few more episodes, just to be sure this one wasn't an anomaly, and the next few episodes were no different than the first.*

Most well-intentioned parents would probably include the ABC Family channel on their "approved" list for teenage viewing. As I mentioned earlier, the name of the channel alone implies wholesome programming. Also, *Pretty Little Liars* has a TV-14 rating, which seems innocuous. Yet I'd argue that this rating is misleading. I considered the four teenage girls (ages fourteen to seventeen) in the small group

---

*Much to my husband's eye-rolling dismay. After five episodes, though, I lost interest and reverted back to rewatching *Friday Night Lights*.

I lead. Would I feel comfortable watching this show with them? Or even knowing they watch the show? Not one bit. They are strong Christians from great families and are leaders in our youth group. Even knowing their maturity level, I also know how impressionable their minds are at this stage of their development. And I, a woman in my midthirties, had to stay on guard as I watched the show so that I knew I was processing sexual content appropriately.

As I researched *Pretty Little Liars*, ABC Family, and similar shows and channels, I was honestly a little surprised at how much effort is dedicated to intentionally marketing these programs to teen girls. The TV show previews hit all the heartstrings: cute boys, friends, and fitting in at school. The commercials are all about pretty shoes, facial cleanser for acne, shampoo, and makeup. On the surface, a TV-14 show on a family channel wouldn't cause me to bat an eye. Knowing what I know now, I hope more parents are aware of how dangerous these seemingly "innocent" or "age-appropriate" shows actually are to brains that aren't adequately developed to process their sexual content.

Still need some convincing? Watchmojo.com has a list of the top ten shows you shouldn't watch with your parents.[8] I know the high schoolers in the youth group Tim pastors watch at least half of these shows. If you think your kids are not watching them, you may be right. But it's likely a friend of theirs is, and your child is probably hearing about it.

Movies

Although children and teens spend less time watching movies than they do TV, parents need to be *more* on guard when it comes to movie content. A study conducted in 1999 reports that 80 percent of all movies shown on network or cable television include sexual content, and oftentimes the content is more explicit[9] than the theatrical release of the movie.[10] This study was released before streaming services like Netflix, Hulu, Vudu, and Amazon Prime existed. Now pretty much any TV or Blu-ray player comes standard with these services.

Recently, the movie *The Wolf of Wall Street* showed up in the new release section on Netflix and Amazon Prime. When the movie released in theaters, an acquaintance of mine saw it with her boyfriend, neither of whom are professing Christians or churchgoers. Sexually explicit material generally doesn't bother them. She mentioned in passing how "dirty" she felt after seeing it and wondered how it was allowed in theatres with an R rating. "It should have been an NC-17, at least," she commented. A crew member on the film agreed in an interview: "Even *I* couldn't believe that they gave it to us. It probably should have been an NC-17."[11]

Kids-in-mind.com is a great resource that allows you to check out the content of movies before seeing them (or letting your kids see them). It rates sex, violence/gore, and language on a scale of 1 (minor) to 10 (extreme). *The Wolf of Wall Street* was rated a 10.4.10, respectively. On a computer or tablet without filters, this kind of movie is readily available to stream with just a couple clicks.

It's not only the extreme R-rated movies that should concern us, especially when it comes to what our children are watching. In a 2006–2009 study of 122 "family" films (rated G, PG, and PG-13), a quarter of female characters (whether cartoon or human) were depicted in "sexy, tight, or alluring attire." Another study found that women in G-rated films are as skimpily clad as women in R-rated films.[12]

Think of most of the cartoon princesses in the last two decades. I remember asking my mom why Ariel from *The Little Mermaid* could wear a bikini top but I couldn't. Media expert Hope Schreiber compiled a list of some hidden and some not-so-hidden sexual references in G- and PG-rated films.[13] When I was in high school, I recall sitting in the locker room with my basketball teammates discussing some of these sexual references, like the minister's erection in the wedding scene of *The Little Mermaid* and Aladdin whispering, "All good teenagers take off your clothes." In a more recent movie, *Ratatouille*, critic Anton Ego makes an oral sex joke by saying (to Linguini, about his food), "If I don't love it, I don't swallow." In *Shrek*, the magic mirror speaks of Snow White, "Just because she lives with seven men doesn't mean she's easy." Yes, that may go over a six-year-old's head, but it doesn't miss their ears (or ours).

Sexual content in films is pervasive, explicit, and accepted without consequence. Unrealistic depictions of women's bodies negatively impact the way viewers assign value and worth to women in real life. Children are consuming and digesting these messages—likely thousands of them each year. While not all are overtly sexual, at minimum these messages objectify our bodies (women's bodies in particular) and do not represent God's design for sexuality.

Music

Music has always been the artist's emotional exploratory sandbox. Songwriters take the mundane and extreme and condense grand philosophical ideas into a brief, poetic form. Songs are the sound track to our daily lives. Music stirs emotion and nostalgia. Lyrics inspire us, console us, inform us, and connect us to universal questions and longings. And in many ways they connect us to one another.

However, sometimes a song isn't intended to delve into the depths of the human psyche, but instead is simply a reflection of the songwriter's culture. (This is my polite way of saying sometimes music reflects the terrible aspects of society—drugs, rape, violence, and irresponsible sex.) It glorifies the more appalling behaviors of human beings.

As a preacher's kid, I wasn't allowed to listen to mainstream music (my father, however, had a few ABBA and Neil Diamond albums hidden in his office at the church). Amy Grant was about as crazy as it got. My first concert was the contemporary Christian artist Carman at the age of nine, and I walked away with my first tape, *Revival in the Land*.* When I turned thirteen, I got my very own stereo with a CD player and my first two CDs: DC Talk's *Jesus Freak* and Jars of Clay's self-titled album.

But even with my parents' strict rules and complete control over what music I brought into the house (I was only allowed to buy music from the local Christian bookstore), I was able to skirt their restrictions and appease my teenage desire to fit in with my classmates. My CD/stereo also dubbed tapes, so while I would make copies of my Christian albums for my friends (yes, I pirated my *Christian* music as a teenager), I'd also sneak blank tapes to my friends so they could copy their mainstream music for me. I'll never forget the time I went on a road trip vacation with my family, my red Sony Walkman attached to my hip. The tape inside had a handmade label that read "DC Talk Mix Tape," but I was actually listening to Metallica's "Enter Sandman." Instead of hearing "What if

---

*My mom's purse also was stolen at that concert.

I stumble, what if I fall?," I was listening to the angst-ridden lyrics "Dreams of wars, dreams of liars."

Following my obsession with Metallica, I gravitated toward a love of country music and rap music, from Diamond Rio and Reba to Snoop Dogg and Tupac. My parents were clueless. Preachers' kids are sneaky.

After church camp my freshman year of high school, I felt compelled to recommit myself to Christ and be rid of the secular influences in my life. My best friend and I collected all our "non-Christian" CDs, drove to the parking lot of a Hastings Entertainment store (poetic justice), and ran over them with her parents' car. We took what little money we had and bought Christian alternatives—The Gaithers (southern gospel) and D.O.C. (Disciples of Christ, a Christian rap group)—to replace what we had destroyed.

Today, my iPod playlist includes a mix of everything from Hillsong to Taylor Swift. (Yes, yes, I know. I know. I'm sorry.) Even the rogue "f-bomb" makes an appearance in a Mumford and Sons song or two. Back in my Metallica days, I would have insisted that lyrics didn't matter. But now, as an adult—and an adult who listens to a diverse playlist—I would argue with my high school self and say yes, lyrics *do* make a difference. Even as an adult, I have to be careful how I interpret and process the things I hear. If my mind starts going down an inappropriate path, then I know it's time to change the station.

What messages do our children consume when they listen to mainstream music? What do these messages teach them about values? And what do kids these days listen to? Using my Teen Choice Awards standard, I've taken the liberty to pull lyrics from two of the winning songs: "Second guessin', but should've hit that" from Demi Lovato's "Really Don't Care" and "There's a million yous baby boo" from Ariana Grande's "Problem."

A quick glance at the nominees for the 2014 Teen Choice Awards was equally troubling. One song in particular, "Turn Down for What" by DJ Snake and Lil Jon, caught my eye. I first heard this song at a church camp—and a relatively conservative one at that. Each night an online radio station played over the loudspeakers as the teens filed into the auditorium for worship services, and "Turn Down for What" was broadcast almost every night. I found the song's beat and words a little annoying (what *were* they saying anyway?), and later, curious whether a contemporary Christian artist was behind these simple and seemingly pointless lyrics, I Googled the song and, like many kids often do, watched the video. I discovered that while the song's few lyrics were mainly about staying high and drunk, the song's music video proved shocking in both vulgar and immature ways.

I don't know how many kids at that church camp did the same (or watched the video simply because it was a popular song), but if they did, they saw a man falling through an apartment building, breaking things and hitting people with his exaggerated-in-size penis, as well as women being treated (and performing) like sex objects.

Please, for the love of Pete, do not watch this video. Let this snippet from an interview with the director suffice:

There were three questions I had after watching "Turn Down for What" for the first time. One, how did the special effects team so realistically depict their protagonist smashing stuff with his penis; two, who are the complete freakazoids that directed this thing; and three, what does it all mean?[14]

And, yes, my parent-friends, this song was nominated for a Teen Choice Award in 2014. Teen. Choice. Award.

Studies show lyrics influence behavior, plain and simple. A study of ninth graders demonstrated that those exposed to sexual lyrics (students averaged 14.7 hours per week listening to songs with sexual content) were two times more likely to engage in sexual intercourse during their freshman year.[15]

Another study on why lyrics matter states:

> Degrading sexual lyrics are more likely to focus on casual sex, "boys being boys," and women's primary usefulness as objects for sexual pleasure. . . . This study's findings are consistent with the theory that teens learn important cues about sexual behavior from media.[16]

It's no surprise that music has always been a staple in the life of a teenager. With each generation comes a new style and anthem for freedom. *This generation is different. You are different. Explore the depths of who you are and find what is yours. This is your time. This is your music. This is your cry.* Music is a rite of passage. It's personal. And it's also extremely easy to enjoy without ever really noticing what it's saying to us. Now's a good time to explore what the songs your family listens to are communicating about sex.

Video Games

Remember *Tetris*? The super-cute *Super Mario Bros*? *Sonic the Hedgehog*? Even the *Street Fighter* days of yore pale in comparison to many mainstream video games this decade.

In the early 1970s, adult consumers were fascinated by the video game *Pong*, but sadly, when the game didn't change much, the cool factor diminished considerably during the

1980s. What happens when you insert sex and violence into a medium? Sales! Skyrocketing sales. And that's exactly what happened in the late 1980s and early 1990s (and continues today).[17] Video games, along with the rest of mainstream media, have become much more sexualized.

We largely determine which video games are appropriate for our kids in the same way we deem which movies are appropriate: we pay attention to the label and the rating, rather than the "fine print" or the details. We accept what the Entertainment Software Ratings Board (ESRB) determines as "kid-friendly" at face value. For example, you probably feel like it's a safe bet to buy your tween or teen an E10+ (Everyone 10 years old and older) or a T (Teen) game, but let's take a closer look at how the ESRB qualifies their ratings:

RATING:	AGE DESCRIPTION:
Early Childhood (EC)	Age 3 and older. No inappropriate content.
Everyone (E)	Age 6 and older. May have minimal violence and language.
Everyone 10 and Older (E10+)	Age 10 and older. Mild violence, mild language, and minimally suggestive themes.
Teen (T)	Age 13 and older. Violence, suggestive themes, crude humor, minimal blood, infrequent strong language.
Mature (M)	Age 17 and older. Intense violence, blood and gore, sexual content, strong language.
Adults Only (AO)	Age 18 and older. Prolonged scenes of intense violence and/or graphic sexual content and nudity.[18]

I recently visited the ESRB's website (esrb.org) specifically to look at the sexual content of games rated for children under seventeen. Here are a few examples from the site:

Game: *Story of Seasons* (E10+)

Synopsis: This is a farming simulation/role-playing game in which players tend to animals, grow crops, and mingle with other farmers and friends. Some story lines reference violence: "[Y]ou went into her room, talked to her, then hit her in the head with a blunt object and killed her," and "After you killed her, you dragged her body to the balcony." Scenes also contain sexually suggestive talk.[19]

Game: *Etrian Mystery Dungeon* (E10+)

Synopsis: This role-playing game allows players to guide a group of adventurers on a mission to save a town from monsters. Players investigate labyrinths and fight fictional creatures, such as giant insects and carnivorous plants. Some female characters sport clothing that reveals large amounts of cleavage. The game contains brief references to alcohol, as well as some foul language.[20]

Game: *Dark Souls II* (T)

Synopsis: Some scenes in the game depict blood and gore: a giant snake boss holds its detached head; a giant boss creature is composed of hundreds of corpses; dead ogres lay by a pool of blood; a torture device is streaked with blood. A boss creature is partially topless, with only her hair covering her breasts. Several vulgar words also appear.[21]

Game: *Omega Quintet* (T)

Synopsis: Players in this role-playing game adopt the roles of warriors battling an evil force. The game contains some suggestive material, including "costume breaks" in which characters are depicted in their underwear and several characters are topless, with steam covering their breasts. Several scenes refer to and depict drunkenness, and in one a character asks, "Could you not spread your alcoholic breath around first thing in the morning?" Swear words are common.[22]

Although it is rated M for Mature (17+), *Grand Theft Auto*, one of the most popular games, is frequently purchased by minors (or acquired for minors by their parents). My husband was recently selling his Xbox One, and in a response he received from Craigslist, a twelve-year-old wanted to trade him *Grand Theft Auto* for one of Tim's games. Concerned, Tim called the number and asked for one of his parents. The conversation went something like this:

Tim: "Hi. I was trying to trade a video game with your son. He wanted to trade *Grand Theft Auto* for mine. Are you aware of what content it has?"

Mom: "Yes, whatever. It's his game. I don't care. He can do what he wants."

ESRB says this about *Grand Theft Auto V*, the most recent version of the game: "The game includes depictions of sexual material/activity: implied fellatio and masturbation; various sex acts (sometimes from a close-up perspective) that the player's character procures from a prostitute—while no nudity is depicted in these sequences, various sexual moaning sounds can be heard."[23]

As I stated earlier in the television section, you may not be purchasing these games for your children, but chances are that they're going to have friends who own them. Don't hide these cultural commonalities from your kids, hoping they won't come across them just because you don't allow them in your own home. Talk to your kids about these kinds of video games and other mainstream media. Teach them how to process sexual material when they come across it . . . because they will.

Having the Conversation

Out of all the conversations you'll have with your child about sex, the conversation about media should be the easiest for you, but it might be the most challenging for your child to hear. You have the advantage of maturity (and now some pretty consistent and revealing statistics). Your child is dealing with hormones and peer pressure. They are also just beginning to understand feelings of desire and grapple with a yearning to connect and belong.

Do you remember what it was like to be fifteen years old? I do. I thought I was *way* more mature and sophisticated than I actually was. My parents were old-fashioned; they didn't know what was *really* going on in the world or in my life. Surely they didn't understand my passion for being culturally well rounded. As a Christian, it was important for me to "become all things to all people so I can save some!" I also lived by the words *Everything is permissible!*—after all, that's what Paul said, right? (The worst teenager is the one armed with years of Vacation Bible School, Awana, and Bible drills. We are always ready to spout Scripture, usually out of context, to prove our point! The four most difficult words you may face from your teen in this conversation are: "But the Bible says . . .")

In hindsight, as adults, we can probably recognize the media influences that impacted us during our teenage years. Some of it wasn't so terrible. Some of it was. Over the years, television shows, movies, and music have shaped my beliefs about love, relationships, morality, values, God, and more. I would even go so far as to say that at times I've allowed media to influence my view of truth—for good and bad.

For example, the media has influenced my definition and understanding of true love. I used to dream I was Meg Ryan in the movies *Sleepless in Seattle* and *You've Got Mail*. She always ended up happy with Tom Hanks, who portrayed the perfect, emotional, generous, and awkwardly cute man. I've since learned that the typical romantic comedy isn't the most accurate reflection of real-life love. The media has also communicated that underage drinking is acceptable and the norm. Even my beloved *Friday Night Lights* depicted how easy it was for high school junior Tim Riggins to buy beer. The more I watched or listened to certain media, the more my vocabulary changed as swear words crept their way into my everyday conversations. Even now, after watching the series *Breaking Bad*, I've somehow picked up Jesse Pinkman's well-known saying, "yo," and use it far too often. The fact is that we digest what we consume. Regardless of our age, we need to be cautious of the media's influence and impact on our lives.

Steps for Talking about Media with Your Kids

1. Look over your family values and determine how they apply to the conversation about media.

Family Values

- We believe God created sex to be a worshipful experience between husband and wife that brings glory to him.
- We believe that because we live in a fallen world and will constantly face distorted views of sexuality, we must learn to identify and process these views in a healthy and biblically sound manner.
- We believe in honest conversation, even if it feels uncomfortable, antiquated, or old-fashioned.
- We believe everybody is created in God's image, and no one should be abused or exploited for any reason.
- We believe we should not be ashamed of sex or sexuality— ever.

- We believe in showing grace, mercy, and love in every circumstance, even toward people whose beliefs we don't agree with
  or understand.
- We believe in the healing and redemptive power of the love of
  God, who sacrificed his Son, Jesus Christ, for our sins.
- We believe in having integrity in our thoughts, words, and actions by demonstrating God's love to everyone, including ourselves, regardless of past or present circumstances.
- We believe in asking for help when we need it.
- We believe in relying on the power of God and prayer, as
  well as being accountable to our family and friends when we
  struggle.

2. **Pick a fun time to talk about media.** Find a good movie,
   TV show, or concert. Enjoy media with your kids. After
   it's over, allow the experience to be a natural lead-in for
   beginning this conversation.

3. **Ask questions.** Ask what music your kids enjoy, what
   their favorite movie of the year was, and what some of
   their favorite television shows are. This isn't so you can
   ascertain how much sexual content they're consuming.
   Listen just to listen. Ask why they like the music, movies, and shows they do. Try to get to the root of why
   particular choices appeal to them. In high school, I was
   drawn to bands with strong female leads (think No
   Doubt and The Cranberries) and bands that expressed a
   lot of pain poetically (Smashing Pumpkins, Jeff Buckley,
   Elliot Smith). I can see now that although I still enjoy
   most of the music I liked when I was in high school,
   back then the hidden pain I harbored from being sexually abused and my desire to feel strong and confident
   undoubtedly informed my choices. Likewise, I secretly
   watched dark movies and television shows my parents
   wouldn't have approved of because I was looking for

characters who wrestled with the same thoughts I had. Talk to your kids about why they are drawn to particular genres. They may have a deeper reason for their choices that needs to be uncovered.

4. **Identify and communicate your family's stance on media consumption.** This is where some "rule making" will come in and where you can expect the most resistance. Now that you understand your kids' why, explain your why to them. Each family will be different. Your restrictions might look more like those of my parents, who were very conservative and moderated everything that came into our home. Or you might be a little more liberal. This is a time for your family to determine what's acceptable, what's not, and why.

6. **Always be open.** Let your child know you're open to discussion if there's something they're interested in that falls outside of the values you've established. This accomplishes a few things: (1) it opens up more trust between you and your kids, and hopefully, they won't feel like they have to sneak around; (2) it helps you gauge what type of media your child or teen is being exposed to and naturally pressured to engage in; and (3) it offers you insights into what your child is being drawn to. If your child presents something really unexpected, then it's probably time to have another conversation and explore the "why" again.

7. **Remember that rules are made to be broken (especially when it comes to teens).** More than likely, even with guidelines in place, your kids are going to break the rules. They'll ride in a car with a friend who listens to that band you absolutely can't tolerate. They'll hear a

song in the mall or see a show or a commercial playing somewhere in public. Chances are, they'll be just like me (and maybe even like you) and intentionally go against your wishes. If you discover your child has broken the media boundaries you've established for your family, be gracious and forgiving (reminding them that you're always open to conversation), and continue to build trust with them.

▶ **THE BOTTOM LINE**

As I mentioned earlier in the chapter, the research is clear: the more a child or teen is exposed to media with sexual content, the more likely they are to have sex at an earlier age. This is frightening, no doubt about it. But all hope is not lost. The studies that also assessed the impact of parental involvement in media choices illustrate a much more positive picture. Yes, the voice of the media is loud, but if you remain understanding, consistent, and communicative, your kids will hear *you* above the noise.

EXPERTS WANT YOU TO KNOW

Olivia Pelts is a trained mental health therapist, a nationally certified counselor, and a licensed professional counselor intern. As an expert in the field of human behavior and performance, she is passionate about issues of trauma, sexuality, and equipping parents to engage their kids in today's culture. Olivia is a graduate of Denver Seminary and currently resides with her husband and their two dogs in St. Petersburg,

Florida, where she maintains a thriving private practice and is actively engaged in CrossFit as a level 1 trainer.

Studies have shown that, in general, children and teens are consuming more media via more platforms (television, the internet, music, etc.) than ever before. Can repeated exposures to hypersexualized messages influence self-esteem and cause young people to develop unrealistic and unhealthy views of sexuality since their brains are still maturing?

Absolutely. There is so much complexity in the brain, particularly in the exchange of dopamine, serotonin, and synaptic wiring/rewiring that occurs when we engage in any type of activity, conversation, or new experience. In fact, research has proven that our brains do not reach full maturation until our mid to late twenties, with the prefrontal cortex (the piece of our brain responsible for high executive processing and decision making) being one of the last sections to develop. So when we ask our teens, "Why can't you just think with your *brain* and not just your emotions?" there is a physiological reason as to why they cannot fully think with their "logical brain," especially if that kind of thinking is not being modeled by you, the parent.

Several years ago, it was estimated that an average individual was exposed to three thousand advertisement messages on a daily basis. With their excessive consumption of social and other media, today's teens are exposed—at a minimum—to double that number, if not more. This barrage of advertising and other messages is impacting their ability to navigate relationships and engage with others. The editor-in-chief of *Advertising Age* estimates that about 8 percent of an ad's message is directly consumed by the conscious mind, while the remaining 92 percent is absorbed by the subconscious, which essentially means we are often not even aware of how the messages we consume shape our beliefs, values, and actions.

When an adolescent boy is exposed to hypersexualized content, his brain signals the reward center to release dopamine, which in turn sends the message: "Hey! This is *awesome*! We want more . . . more . . . *more*." In addiction work, we know it takes only a small initial exposure to be intrigued, but with each subsequent exposure, the brain demands increased stimuli until the cycle erupts into a full-blown addiction. Generally speaking, this will affect the ways in which this adolescent boy will connect with females relationally, as well as his underlying beliefs about female anatomy. And it can result in a skewed interpretation and use of sex. In short, increased exposure to hypersexualized content can create serious intimacy issues and a very emotionally disconnected boy who will eventually become an emotionally and relationally "stuck" grown man.

In 2007, a study conducted by the American Psychological Association concluded that adolescent girls who had been exposed to sexualized images from a young age were more prone to depression, eating disorders, and low self-esteem. When consuming hypersexualized media, young girls see what they are not, which causes serious dissonance within them. Young girls realize they will never be that thin or have large breasts or luxuriously flowing hair, and this realization causes anxiety, depression, and at times, eating disorders, because our culture says these are the types of women men are attracted to. Girls don't see themselves—the way God made them—in the images offered by our culture.

It is ignorant to believe that media consumption has little or no effect on your children. But it's absolutely tragic to acknowledge the power of media and not establish parameters around media consumption in your household, or worse, not engage in conversation about these issues with your children.

We can't always control what our children see or hear. What are some ways a family can communicate positive values to their children to help them process inappropriate or offensive media in a healthy way?

We have to start with ourselves first and ask ourselves, as parents, some serious questions: How do we feel about sex? What do we believe about boundaries and media consumption? What is our body and behavior saying when the topic of pornography or masturbation is broached? Figure out where you stand and what your own values are first so that you can then communicate those values clearly and effectively to your children. Second, remember that each of your children is unique and different and, therefore, must be engaged differently from their siblings. What works with one child may not work with your other children.

We cannot assume our kids' innocence. Children today spend the majority of their awake hours online. A 2010 study by the Kaiser Family Foundation concluded that the average eight- to ten-year-old spends almost eight hours a day engaging with a variety of different media. Older children and teenagers spend more than eleven hours per day. Your child is not the exception to the rule. Statistically, they are the rule.

We can't sex-proof our kids, no matter how hard we try. The "chastity-belt-preaching parents" proclaim legalism, not grace. If we want to connect and communicate with our kids honestly and authentically, and if we want them to come to us with their questions and concerns, we need to offer them grace and openness, not a list of dos and don'ts. Providing your children with a value and belief system through consistent, authentic engagement and boundaries helps inform their decisions and equips them for life. A legalistic list is easily discarded when peer pressure kicks in.

What advice would you give parents to help them understand both the long- and short-term effects of consuming media on children?

The best advice I can offer parents is for them to consider the ways in which they use electronic devices and consume media to "numb out" or in the name of "catching up" on the news or seeing the latest happenings on Facebook. How do you engage with electronics in your home? What does your behavior communicate to your kids? Do you put parameters around your own media consumption, or do you allow it to wreak havoc on your personal life by fueling envy or creating emotional imbalance and "fear of missing out" syndrome?

Remember, kids learn how to socialize and engage
by observing and emulating you and others in their
environment, so think first about your own media use and
the message it's sending to your kids.

Second, and I can't say this enough: boundaries.
Boundaries. Boundaries. Create some family rules
regarding media consumption and electronic usage. One
of the most loving things you can do for your child is to
limit their screen time. Video games should not be played
more than one to two hours a day. Get a basket and at 6
p.m. every evening, put all electronics—including your
own—in the basket (either for an allotted time or for the
rest of the evening). This will allow you all to engage
with one another without being interrupted by someone
tweeting, snapping, or playing. Better yet, make one day
a week "screen free," and use some of this time to engage
with your kids.

Also consider whether or not you might be using media
or electronics as a babysitter or entertainment for your
children. If you're routinely placing an iPad in your kids'
hands when you go to the doctor's office or out to lunch
with a friend, you are communicating a powerful message:
"I am too busy or distracted to engage with you. Children
are to be seen and not heard."

Will these boundaries limit you, as the parent, in some
ways? Absolutely. You might find you have to work a little
bit at creatively engaging with your kids. But continually
ask yourself this question to help keep your priorities
on track: Am I in it for the short-term reprieve or for the
long-term benefits? Remember, you have the power to
shape and mold your child's mind and heart. You have the

ability to teach them how to think intellectually, connect emotionally, and engage in healthy relationships with others.

Every day, almost minute by minute, you have the opportunity to show up and be present for your kids. The gift of yourself, here and now, is one of the most long-lasting and loving gifts you can give your children.

4

Google Is the New Sex Ed

The Impact of Pornography on the Brain and the World

You're sitting in the car at a stoplight (a very long stoplight and you're behind fifty other cars, so you're not driving, of course!). A song comes on the radio, and you want to know who sings it. What do you do?

Or maybe you want to locate the closest pharmacy. Or you need to find out if that cactus your new puppy ate is poisonous. Where do you look for the information?

If you're anything like me, or most of the developed world's population, you turn to Google (or, to be fair, any other search engine you can access on your phone). Anything you need to know you can find by typing a few words and pressing search. Pages of information appear within seconds. You don't even need to be connected to a computer. Most of us can access anything the internet offers by using the phones in our purses or pockets.

The hard truth is that search engines have usurped parents' roles in the sexual education of their children. Often, by the time well-intentioned parents initiate "the talk," their kids have already researched their questions about sex on their own via Google or another search engine. Case in point: the conversations I had with a number of girls at summer camps in 2013 revealed the same truth again and again. They'd learned about sex on the internet, more often than not via Google Images:

> Teen: "So, I've never told anyone this, but I look at bad stuff on the internet."
> Me: "What do you mean by 'bad stuff'?"
> Teen: "Naked pictures. You know. Porn."
> Me: "How long have you been looking?"
> Teen: "I first saw porn when I was ten years old. I was looking up what _____ meant."
> Me: "How did you look it up?"
> Teen: "Google. Well, Google Images. Because it's just right there and it's faster."

Why am I not surprised? Although it's been almost twenty years, that's *exactly* what I did when I had a question about sex. Granted, Google didn't exist in the midnineties, but I still typed s-e-x into a search engine and went exploring. It makes perfect sense. When we need information, we look it up on the internet. Our kids know this. Why wouldn't they follow suit?

It's Not Just Google

I don't want to pick a fight with Google. It's not the company's fault, and it even has safety measures in place to help filter out inappropriate search results (see Resources for the Conversation). It has recently taken a strict stance against pornography in advertising too. Although Google is the most common search engine, it's not the only place kids go when they want to look at pornography.

Just about any social media app or website—Twitter, Facebook, Instagram, YouTube, Vine, Snapchat, Periscope, even Pinterest—is a potential avenue through which to access porn (remember the Kim Kardashian photos on Instagram we discussed?). Although these companies have terms of use that prohibit posting explicit photos or videos, when the content is almost exclusively user-generated, it's not going to be clean. Type "sex" into any of these social media apps or even just click on a popular nonsexual hashtag, and I guarantee you'll find something sexual. People use trending news stories and hashtags on social media to distribute porn to unsuspecting users all the time. An innocent click on something like #elections can bring up pornography in mere seconds (please don't try this at home).

This month, one of the young men my husband mentors mentioned the app Whisper in conversation. It gained some notoriety when a gun threat on a similar app, After School, prompted a school to increase security. The person wrote, "I actually brought the gun today, yall lucky yall alive. Just wait until Thursday. First target is the main office, then any other victims I can get. Yall think I'm kidding. I'm going to laugh at yalls funerals."[1]

Both apps allow users to create and post content anonymously. Knowing I was collecting data for this book, Tim
suggested I take a look at them, but when I searched for
"After School," the app store yielded no results. I found
out later that Apple had removed the app due to "sexually explicit content." The Whisper app, however, was still
available, so I downloaded it and planned to explore it a
few days later.

Two days after I installed the app, I was surprised to receive a notification that someone had "whispered," despite
the fact that I hadn't created an account or even opened
the app yet. When I opened the notification, an image of a
first-place ribbon filled the screen, with the text: "Who has
the best rack? Winner gets a prize!"

Evidently I'd received the notification because the person
who had sent me the message was nearby (I had location
services turned on in my phone). The whisper was a call to
action challenging women to post photos of their breasts
to be judged by the user. Unable to resist a play on words,
I rushed to post the first reply: an image of a very impres-
sive gun rack with text that read, "I win." The app created
an account name for me at that point—I had no choice in
it—and posted my snarky response.

I showed Tim, explained to him what had happened, and
promptly deleted the app off my phone. Although I didn't see
any images worthy of an R rating (or worse), the potential
was clearly there.

It's not just search engines and apps. Junk email promises
men anatomical "enhancements," and pornographers send
unsolicited mail with attachments, viruses, and photos that
can end up on any computer, including the one your child

uses. As much as I know about avoiding pornography on the internet, and even with the software I have installed on my computer, I still see it (unintentionally) from time to time.

Once, while I was performing some routine maintenance on my blog, I checked out which websites had linked to it and noticed that an article I'd written recently had garnered a lot of traffic from one site in particular. The website had an innocent-enough URL, so I clicked it, not thinking twice. Boom! As I sat in the middle of a busy coffee shop, my computer screen was suddenly flooded with pornographic images. I quickly closed the windows, embarrassed at what had happened, and told Tim. Not only had I seen the images, so had everyone who was sitting behind me. I was horrified.

Exposure to online pornography happens to almost everyone. Even if we take every precaution to avoid it, it is the one conversation we can't avoid. We must be proactive.

A Brief History of Mainstream American Pornography

Let's switch gears for a moment. Although we are mainly talking about internet pornography in this chapter, it's important to understand the big picture, which includes the history of pornography in westernized cultures.

Before the internet, people accessed mainstream pornography mostly via magazines like *Playboy*, *Penthouse*, and *Hustler*. First published in 1953, *Playboy* was considered soft-core pornography. It usually included women who were only topless and never depicted full views of genitals or sex acts. Before long, though, *Playboy* wasn't extreme enough

147

for some men. When *Penthouse* released in the United States in 1969,[2] it pushed society's boundaries:

> Whereas *Playboy* bared breasts in the midfifties, now *Penthouse* has introduced pubic hair . . . and kinky letters to the editor on subjects like caning and slave parties.[3]

Because *Playboy* and *Penthouse* targeted different audiences, the two magazines didn't compete. *Penthouse* continued to publish more explicit material, while *Playboy* unapologetically remained true to its self-defined "classy" image and kept consistent with its "girl next door" look. The fact that *Playboy* and *Penthouse* targeted two different audiences left ample space in the industry for someone to take print pornography to the next extreme.

Within three and a half years of the initial publication of *Hustler* in 1974, more than three million people subscribed to the magazine, generating a profit of more than $13 million annually. "Anyone can be a playboy and have a penthouse," *Hustler* creator Larry Flynt said, "but it takes a man to be a Hustler."[4]

Hustler's mission was to be as explicit as possible. Flynt was quoted as saying *Playboy* and *Penthouse* paved the way for his *Hustler* to be the "first nationally distributed magazine to show [inside of female genitalia]."[5]

The availability and accessibly of internet pornography has dramatically impacted sales of magazines like *Playboy*, *Penthouse*, and *Hustler*. While they are still in print, subscriptions are at only a fraction of what they once were. The company that owns *Penthouse* filed for bankruptcy protection in 2013, and Flynt says he predicts *Hustler* will be out of print soon. *Playboy* has also stopped printing images of fully nude women.

The Present State of Internet Pornography

It was difficult to write this section, and we'll keep it brief because I don't want to expose you unnecessarily to the horrors of online pornography. At the same time, if I simply said, "Porn is becoming more extreme," and moved on, that statement means nothing if you don't have a reference point from which to begin.

Because of anonymity and the lack of regulation in both publishing and viewing porn, the internet is home to some of the most extreme imagery imaginable. In fact, it's *beyond* extreme now. According to a porn producer, "This is an industry running out of ideas."[6] Just as *Penthouse* tried to outdo *Playboy* and *Hustler* tried to outdo *Penthouse*, internet porn producers create the most excessively gratuitous content possible to garner the most web traffic and revenue.

Whereas pornography in the 1950s was more or less comprised of nude pinup models, today it's a very different story. Images of graphic sex between one woman and as many as nine men (or any combination of genders) is not out of the ordinary. Anal sex, sex with animals, and even incest is also depicted regularly and leaves nothing to the imagination. Pornography involving children is rampant, even though it carries significant legal consequences. Websites cater to those who wish to view pornographic images involving dead bodies (necrophilia). Pornography has many pockets of fetishes and fantasy, including those depicting violent acts like rape, kidnapping, and even murder. According to Gail Dines, "Porn plays out 'fantasy' sex that looks more like sexual assault than making love."[7]

These are not pleasant images to think about, but they are the reality. And if we don't have an understanding of exactly what we're dealing with, then we're less likely to find effective ways to address the problem.

Your Children and Porn: The Stats

According to the US Department of Justice, "Never before in the history of telecommunications media in the United States has so much indecent (and obscene) material been so easily accessible by so many minors in so many American homes with so few restrictions."[8]

While researching very basic statistics (e.g., at what age the average child is first exposed to porn or how frequently children within a certain age range visit pornographic sites online), I discovered most of the current research is already, on average, two years old. In contrast to research published five to seven years ago, children are exposed to and accessing more pornography, and at a younger age, than in years past.

Although I will attempt to ensure this book cites the most current statistics at the time of its publication, know it is likely, based on statistical history and technological advances, that these statistics may not reflect the most up-to-date details. I wish I could look into the future and see which new apps are being developed or what the next big "thing" will be online, but I can't. I encourage you to visit my website 5ThingsBook.com, and I will do my best to update it with the latest information and resources.

I've spent hours researching the average age children today are exposed to pornography, but there is little scientific data, and much of what does exist offers conflicting information. For example, some studies cite the average age as eight years old, others say eleven years old, and another study says fourteen years old. One common conclusion reached by all the studies is that the older a child is, the more sexually curious they are. An eight-year-old (or younger) child may accidentally click on a link or unintentionally pull up a pornographic website. An older child is more likely to seek out inappropriate material, at first to satisfy curiosity, then later for sexual enjoyment.

In 2012, Tru Research conducted 2,017 online interviews with teens, ages thirteen to seventeen, and parents of teens. Their research showed:

- Seventy percent of teens hide their online behavior from their parents, up from 45 percent in 2010. (I recently unscientifically polled about twenty girls from our youth group. One hundred percent said they hide something online from their parents.)
- Half of teens said they would change their online behavior if they knew their parents were watching.

So how do teens hide their online behavior?

- Clear the browser history (53 percent)
- Close/minimize browser when a parent walks in (46 percent)
- Hide or delete instant messages or videos (34 percent)
- Lie or omit details about online activities (23 percent)
- Use a computer parents don't check (23 percent)
- Use an internet-enabled mobile device (21 percent)
- Use privacy settings to make certain content viewable only by friends (20 percent)
- Use private browsing modes (20 percent)

- Create a private email address unknown to parents (15 percent)
- Create duplicate/fake social network profiles (9 percent)[9]

In 2001 (please note the date on this—fifteen years ago! This is in a premobile era!), a study by the Kaiser Family Foundation discovered that among all youth ages fifteen to seventeen, 70 percent say they have accidentally stumbled across pornography online.[10]

I wish I could paint a different picture, that somehow your child is immune from seeing pornography. However, I continue to hear *from children* that they not only have seen porn (sometimes accidentally) but also cannot stop looking at it. Because of the way our brains are designed, this is the perfect plan for the enemy to destroy this and future generations.

This Is Your Brain on Porn

Some people consider pornography harmless. Using pornography is even a commonly celebrated rite of passage for men in our culture. (And I use the word *common* instead of the word *normal*. I don't think looking at pornography is normal, but it is certainly commonplace. That distinction is key.) How many television shows and movies reference it casually? It is no longer considered taboo in mainstream culture.

But pornography isn't as harmless as our society makes it out to be. It can affect everything from how our brains function to the health of our relationships. In addition to the fact that it's not a healthy or moral way to experience sexuality, using pornography can cause long-term psychological and sexual complications like violent behavior, impotence, inability to orgasm later in life without the assistance of pornography, and addictive and compulsive sexual behaviors. And, over time, viewing sexual images can impact and change the way the brain processes information, as we'll see later in this chapter.

Let's start at the beginning. How are young men and women affected by accidental exposures to pornography or generally sexualized images in the media? Males and females are wired differently when it comes to responding to sexual imagery. Generally speaking, males are aroused by what they see,[11] but that doesn't mean women are immune to having a physical or sexual response to attractiveness or sensual imagery. When our brains receive sexualized images and don't know how (or are not developmentally mature enough) to process them, we slowly begin to believe the story they tell us.

For example, young men are bombarded with a barrage of sexual images in everyday life. During a simple walk through the mall they will see many images of airbrushed bodies, large breasts, and come-hither looks. If a young man is not developmentally mature enough to process those images in a healthy and biblical way, they will replay again and again in his mind. He might think of them while masturbating, and eventually, they will color the way he sees all women.

Those same images, along with the knowledge that the young men in their lives have seen them too, also impact young women. If a young woman is unable to process the images appropriately, she will likely begin to write her own story about the qualities that define her as "beautiful," as well as how she should dress, look, and act to meet those expectations and win the attention of guys.

However, if a man is psychologically and spiritually equipped to see an arousing image, he might think, *Hey, there's a really attractive picture. That person's created in the image of God, just like me. Whatever I am feeling biologically (aroused, excited, etc.) is totally normal. But my brain knows this image isn't an accurate portrayal of reality.* That's a healthy response, and it's a thought pattern that can be learned, through practice, over time.

If a girl has been taught to see the truth in sexualized images, she might think, *There's a really attractive image. That person's created in the image of God, just like me. I know true attractiveness doesn't mean perfection, and I don't need to mimic society's standard of beauty.* Again, this is a healthy response and is a thought pattern that can be practiced and learned over time.

"We don't really talk about sex, we just see it all over the place," observes Ran Gavrieli, a gender studies scholar at Tel Aviv University. "Our history of silence never did any good. Young girls get the message, not only from hardcore porn but from our porn-influenced mainstream culture. Have you seen any Miley Cyrus or Lady Gaga video clips or commercials? That's porn with clothes on. [Girls] learn if you want to be worthy of love, you have to be worthy of sexual desire."[12]

Gavrieli makes an important point: porn doesn't have to include nudity. Daily we're faced with images that are, as he so aptly states, "porn with clothes on."

For me, looking at porn as a teen and a young adult was definitely both emotional/mental and biological/sexual. I initially looked up sex on the internet for educational purposes, but then continued to be drawn back in. On one level, I saw those sexual images as a teacher, offering instruction in the ways I needed to look and act in order to be loved. At the same time, being sixteen, I was sexually developed enough to respond biologically to what I was seeing. While researching this book, I had to be extremely cautious. Although I wasn't searching out pornography, some of the research contained explicit descriptions, and at times I noticed I was beginning to respond biologically. *That is just the way we are wired.* I needed to walk away and regain my perspective. In short: I was (or was going to be) aroused and knew that wasn't what God intended for me, so I changed the channel in my mind and removed myself from the situation.

Nobody ever told me arousal was a natural part of growing up and developing sexually. Remember, in my mind, because I wasn't married, feeling something sexual was bad. Regardless of anything I tried to do, I still had a sexual response to the images I was consuming. I didn't know that by repeatedly viewing those images on the computer screen, my brain was chemically and physically changing, which over time would make it all the more difficult to stop.

"Our kids aren't just internalizing messages about what sex is like when they watch porn uncritically," observes author and sexuality educator Al Vernacchio. "They're also internalizing very skewed messages about what it means to be a man or a woman, about the place of violence in sexual activity, and about how dehumanizing sex can be. None of these messages are healthy ones, so we *have* to be able to counter them."[13]

So what happens when someone goes from the occasional or accidental exposure to porn to a regular habit of viewing it? Studies show the effects of pornography on the brain are similar to the effects of substances like heroin or alcohol. Viewing pornography can trigger the release of the brain's "pleasure chemicals"—dopamine, serotonin, norepinephrine, and others. You know the rush you feel during or after a workout or while tasting a bite of chocolate ice cream or helping a friend in need? That rush is caused by the pleasure chemicals in your brain saying, "Hey, this is good. Keep doing this." It's a biological reward system that both reinforces the things we need for survival and reminds us to enjoy the good things in life.

Unfortunately, drugs, alcohol, and even food or unhealthy relationships can fool your brain. After doing whatever your brain interprets as something that "feels good," it sends the message, "Please, do more of this! You need this!" Over time, the brain needs more of these pleasure chemicals to feel the same rush, so we revisit the unhealthy habit more often or in greater quantities.

Functional MRI testing reveals that when a person looks at porn (intentionally or not), because "mating" is part of our primal survival skills, the brain responds as if the person is seeing a positive image.[14] Coupling the brain's response to porn with the flood of pleasure chemicals amounts to a double whammy. Over time, the brain gets the message: "You need the release pornography brings in order to survive."

Studies demonstrate that teens experience the "reward pathway" at a level two to four times higher than adults, which means their brains release much more dopamine and other pleasure chemicals at a faster rate.[15] Thus, with children and teenagers, the risk of forming addictive behaviors is even greater than that of adults.

If and when a person attempts to quit looking at porn, they will often feel stressed, depressed, or tired because the brain has grown accustomed to the flood of feel-good chemicals that have now been taken away. The reward system has been restructured so that normal everyday activities—like socializing with friends or family, performing well on the job, playing a sport, enjoying a movie, or doing any hobby that used to bring great satisfaction—don't even register as pleasure in the brain anymore.

This cycle explains so much of my own struggle with pornography. What began innocently evolved into a cycle that was magnified in my off-screen relationships with men in my late teens and early twenties. Even into my late twenties and early thirties, at my most stressed times, I would find myself on a destructive path. What would begin as innocent online clothes shopping often ended in an attempt to seek out (and at times, find and use) pornography.*

I'm not alone in this. A girl I mentor, Carly, is a student at Moody Bible Institute. "When I was in third grade, I was molested, and was sexually abused and sexually harassed throughout my childhood," she told me. "Then, in sixth grade, I searched the word 'sex' in Google. I wanted to know what happened to me when I was abused, so I looked it up out of curiosity. But that curiosity soon became like an addiction. I knew at the time that what happened wasn't right. My compulsive pornography viewing lasted seven years and was very destructive in every area of my life."

The Good News: The Brain Can Be Rewired

The good news is that neural pathways are not necessarily permanent; our brains can actually be rewired. Teens are at

---

*I have been extra cautious in doing my research for this book, only accidentally stumbling on explicit content a handful of times. Each time I immediately told my husband and a friend. Most of the research I've done has been humbling and confirming in my decision to never again seek out pornography.

risk for developing addictive behaviors more quickly than adults, but on the flip side, because their brains are still forming, rewiring their neural synapses happens much faster than it typically does for adults. Although they may get hooked faster, teenage brains heal faster too.

At the height of my pornography viewing, if you had told me there would come a time when I would be repulsed by it, I wouldn't have believed you. Looking at porn was so wired into my brain, I couldn't fathom life without it. But after confessing, praying daily, serving my church, getting counseling, installing accountability software, and practicing other coping mechanisms when I am stressed,* I have progressed to the point that even the thought of looking at porn disgusts me.

When we can see and comprehend that pornography isn't real, when we understand the personal and global implications of viewing it (more on this in the next section), and when we practice other coping mechanisms, we can rewire our brains to respond to healthier stimuli. Many studies in the last twenty years have consistently shown that because of the way our brains are wired for addiction or compulsive behavior, by practicing the opposite through processes and behaviors, our brains can rewire back to the way God intended. It's not easy, but it's possible.

What You Need to Know about Pornography's Global Impact

It's important for you and your child to understand the dire impact pornography can have personally, but it's also impor-

---

*When I get stressed now, I go for a long walk or a quick run, or I punch and kick cardboard boxes in our garage.

tant to look at the big picture. The pornography industry has a grave global impact that reaches far beyond Western borders. Every time a person chooses to look at porn, they participate in the cycle of supply and demand.

With the explosion of accessibility made possible by the internet, now "the laws of supply and demand have been turned upside down," says Paul Fishbein, founder of the *Adult Video News.* "We're on par to put out 15,000 new releases this year, which is insane."[16] Formal (legally operational) producers can't keep up with the demand, even though they're trying as hard as they can. Free amateur videos are readily available with the click of a mouse, and it's these videos that have increased the demand for sex trafficking.

Those who are pro-pornography, or "porn apologists" as some label them, dismiss the argument that supply and demand fuels sex trafficking and all the illegal and unethical things that coincide with it, including drugs, assault, suicide, and homicide. I admit, there's not a lot of quantitative research to support the claim, because the connection between pornography's cycle of supply and demand and sex trafficking is almost impossible to study. Even a casual porn user believes they are looking at photographs or videos of consenting adults.

Take, for example, the conversation Tim and I had with a friend about his porn use a few days after I had finished reading *Pornland.** Our friend admitted that he didn't see anything wrong with his pornography viewing, as long as it wasn't a compulsive behavior that interfered with his life. "The way I see it," he continued, "I'm watching two

---

*When you're in the middle of writing a book about sexuality, you find having conversations about porn use is a relatively common occurrence.

consenting adults have sex. And even the webcam stuff now, you know, college guys filming their girlfriends or whatever. It's harmless."

"Can I pose a hypothetical for you, informed by stories and research I was reading yesterday?" I asked him, referring to *Pornland*.

"Go for it," he said.

"What if those college guys filming their girlfriends weren't actually college guys filming their girlfriends? What if that's just what the marketers of that site want you to believe? You search for 'college girl sex' and click on a URL because it looks somewhat legit. But what if those 'college girls' were actually forced into the porn industry by human traffickers? And their college boyfriends weren't actually their college boyfriends but instead were cheap porn producers who carefully craft videos and websites so well that you believe you're watching an amateur webcam? And off camera there's a director saying to one of these 'college girls,' 'This man will repeatedly put his [penis] as far down your throat as he can, and at the same time this other man is going to have sex with you, and if you don't scream with pleasure and look like you're enjoying every second of this, we're going to beat you.'

"And then they have to film the act three times so they can record it from different angles, so that girl endures terrible abuse three times under the threat of her life. And she can't speak English very well because she's from Moldova. And she doesn't know where to go to get medical help, because you know those men doing that to her in that way is going to injure her physically. And she's labeled a whore and covered in shame and can only make the pain go away by doing drugs. Then five years later she kills herself because she's trapped in an industry that won't let her go and continually abuses her, and the only way out is for her to take her own life. Is that *really* a 'college girl' having some fun with her boyfriend for a webcam?"

Our friend's voice softened. "That doesn't really happen, does it?"

"Oh, it happens all the time. More than you think. And worse than you think." I could feel my heart racing. Tim gave me a look that said I needed to relax just a little bit.

"I know there's really crazy stuff out on the internet, but I would *never* watch that disgusting stuff," our friend insisted.

I replied a little more calmly, "Well, you might not. But you might. You know that rush you get when you watch whatever porn you watch?"

"Yeah."

"Well, those 'feel good' chemicals in your brain are a biological response to what you're watching. There's nothing you can do to control what your brain does when you watch porn. Eventually, when someone watches porn, their brain needs more of that chemical—dopamine—to feel that same rush. And because of the way our brains work, we'll likely continue moving on to the next extreme."[17]

Remember, the more a person uses porn, the greater the amount and explicitness required to achieve the same level of satisfaction. This means more women and children are becoming commodities in this industry—and being forced to do these things we deem now as "disgusting." Studies prove that for some regular porn users, pornographic acts they found disgusting in the past now turn them on.[18] And as you can imagine, it's harder for the so-called legit porn producers to hire people to do those extreme things. It's much easier—and less expensive—for people to be kidnapped, devalued, dehumanized, and turned into nothing more than sex slaves.

Take, for example, the issue of child pornography. I think it's safe to say we all know that men and women are trafficked and used for porn every day. But what about children? Most of us have heard stories of children trafficked for labor or prostitution. But are children trafficked for pornography?

Child pornography—the documentation of a minor for the purpose of sex—is a reality in our world (and our country) today. As pornography grows more extreme, the child porn industry grows with it. When I look at the keyword searches that bring new visitors to my website, almost daily I see phrases like "child sex," "sex with little girls," and "daughter porn." If this many people stumble across my website by accident in search of child pornography, I can only imagine how vast the traffic is and how strategic those who make money from it are. One would think (and hope) that child pornography would be difficult to find, but statistics prove otherwise. One out of every five pornographic images is of a child. And 55 percent of all child pornography comes from the United States.

In a study of 932 sex addicts, 90 percent of the men and 77 percent of the women indicated that looking at pornography featuring adults "played a significant role in their [child pornography] addiction."[19] These statistics clearly illustrate how regular pornography use can escalate into an addiction to child pornography.

To be honest, before writing this book, I wasn't sure how available child pornography is online. Turns out, it's not as difficult to find as you might think. Not long ago my husband had coffee with James, a college student he mentors, and when he mentioned I was writing this book, James asked if we'd ever heard of the "Deep Web." A few Google searches and YouTube videos later, I learned enough about the Deep Web to know I didn't want to learn any more about it. An article from CNN Money describes it this way:

> It first debuted as *The Onion Routing* project in 2002, made by the U.S. Naval Research Laboratory as a method for communicating online anonymously. Some use it for sensitive communications, including political dissent. But in the last decade, it's also become a hub for black markets that sell or distribute drugs (think Silk Road), stolen credit cards, illegal pornography, pirated media and more. You can even hire assassins.[20]

It sounds too evil to be true, but let me assure you, it is true. I asked two computer programmers to confirm or deny what my surface-level research found. Both have been on the Deep Web and confirmed child pornography is one click away after logging on via an anonymous server. When I viewed a screen grab from a forum where people buy and sell illegally, this was the first posting (I've edited it to make it as clean as possible):

> Best price for a (preferably) 14 year old girl as a sex slave. Virgin if possible. Offering 100BTC-500BTC. Pictures required.

The site uses Bitcoins (BTC) for payment. Bitcoins are anonymous and difficult to trace. One Bitcoin ranges in value, but typically averages from two hundred to three hundred dollars.[21] The person who wanted to buy a fourteen-year-old girl to use as a sex slave was offering approximately $30,000 to $150,000.

It's critical that you talk with your child about porn and sex trafficking. We should be concerned about sex trafficking as a social justice issue, but we also need to help our children understand how they are vulnerable to traffickers. It's easy to imagine tragedies happening around the world, but the hard truth is that children are being trafficked for labor and sex in every state in America. In the United States, estimates suggest that as many as three hundred thousand children may become victims of commercial sexual exploitation each year.[22] It's a profitable business; a pimp can make $150,000 to $200,000 per child each year. The average pimp has four to six girls.[23]

On the US Department of State's website, in the middle of all the statistics and laws and policies, are stories of people who were trafficked. One story features Alissa, who was only sixteen when she met a man at a Dallas convenience store and moved in with him a short time later. Soon afterward, he talked her into becoming an escort and having sex with men for money.

> He took her to an area known for street prostitution and forced her to hand over all of her earnings. He made Alissa get a tattoo of his nicknames, branding her as his property, and he posted prostitution advertisements with her picture on an internet site.[24]

He kept her under his control by threatening and physically assaulting her. He later pled guilty to human trafficking charges for what he did to Alissa.

The link between pornography—and pornography *addiction*—and sex trafficking is obvious. In fact, "The federal Trafficking Victims Protection Act defines human trafficking broadly to encompass a variety of 'commercial sex acts' which include prostitution, pornography and sexual performance," says author Linda Smith, former congresswoman and founder and president of Shared Hope International. "The reality is, any pornography that was produced using an adult who was forced, defrauded or coerced to perform the act or anyone under 18 years old, regardless of force, fraud or coercion, qualifies as sex trafficking. Pornography plays a pivotal role in the commercial sex industry. Traffickers often record the rape of their victims, creating two sources of income: the sale of the live victim and the recording of the act for online viewers."

Although scientific studies are rare, the anecdotal research—the stories of those who have lived to tell about their horrific experiences with sex trafficking—is consistent and heartbreaking. Pornography, the distortion of God's creation of humankind and sex, destroys the fabric of our families. It biologically rewires our brains and our ability to function as he intends us to. It oppresses others, as trafficking and slavery entrap them. It also burdens those who fall victim to its lures. When we help our children understand the multifaceted aspects of porn, the ripple effects echo into eternity. You might assume that the conversations you have with your child about the dangers of pornography can't or won't have a widespread impact, but let me assure you that they can . . . and they will.

Having the Conversation

We've covered a lot of material in this chapter. Here are some points and questions that will help to guide the conversations you have with your child about the internet, pornography, and sex trafficking.

1. **Pair up.** If you're married, sit down with your spouse and determine what needs to happen. Ensure you're on the same page regarding your beliefs about pornography, your personal experience with it, and your goals and hopes for your family and child. I personally recommend writing these things down so you can access them at a future time if necessary. If, in this conversation, you and your spouse can't agree, involve a mediator such as a pastor or a counselor to help you work through the roadblocks.

And if you're not married, it's still important to make the same determinations: What are your beliefs, experiences, and goals? What do you hope for your family? Write down your answers. If you are in a coparenting situation, talk to the child's other parent about this conversation. Involve that person if it's possible and wise to do so. And before you talk to your child, share your thoughts with a friend, another parent, a pastor, or a counselor. They may be able to give you additional insights.

2. **Look over your family values and see how they apply.**

Family Values

- We believe God created sex to be a worshipful experience between husband and wife that brings glory to him.
- We believe that because we live in a fallen world and will constantly face distorted views of sexuality, we must learn to identify and process these views in a healthy and biblically sound manner.
- We believe in honest conversation, even if it feels uncomfortable, antiquated, or old-fashioned.
- We believe everybody is created in God's image, and no one should be abused or exploited for any reason.

- We believe we should not be ashamed of sex or sexuality—ever.
- We believe in showing grace, mercy, and love in every circumstance, even toward people whose beliefs we don't agree with or understand.
- We believe in the healing and redemptive power of the love of God, who sacrificed his Son, Jesus Christ, for our sins.
- We believe in having integrity in our thoughts, words, and actions by demonstrating God's love to everyone, including ourselves, regardless of past or present circumstances.
- We believe in asking for help when we need it.
- We believe in relying on the power of God and prayer, as well as being accountable to our family and friends when we struggle.

3. **Have a family meeting.** Get the whole family together if possible (and age appropriate) to discuss pornography. Before the meeting, write down what you want to tell your kids. Here's a tip: don't try to cover every topic at once. Maybe you need to start with the basics, or maybe pornography is already a concern in your household. Write down what you need to talk about at *this* meeting. Try to stay focused on that topic, but allow questions and circumstances to navigate the conversation.

If you've discovered porn on the computers or other devices in your home, then meet privately with each child, if applicable, to discuss these findings. If you have not found pornography, explain what it is, what it does, and why it's normal to be curious about it. At the same time, describe how looking at pornography impacts their well-being (and also the well-being of others).

Some people suggest having this conversation in a car because it's less awkward—you can avoid eye contact and nobody can go anywhere. However, I think having this conversation face-to-face in your home is best. Try to use humor and compassion to demonstrate that talking about sex is normal. Although it may feel uncomfortable, looking your child in the eyes while you talk about these topics communicates that sex isn't something to be ashamed of talking about. We don't need to have these conversations in secret, or even dread or fear them. Talking about sex is as normal as talking about the latest sports news (okay, it's not *that* normal, but I think you see where I'm going with this).

4. **Respond cautiously.** Hopefully, your conversation won't just entail you talking and your child staring at you traumatized. Remember, it's about them. Ask questions, give them time to answer, and listen. Listen graciously. Prepare ahead of time for the likelihood that you will hear something you weren't expecting. It's okay for you to feel whatever it is you may feel, but use caution when responding to your child. Understand that they may be less willing to talk to you in the future if they believe they are being judged. If your child admits something and asks if you're upset, let them know you need some time to process the information they've conveyed. Always communicate how much you love your child, no matter what they've done.

5. **Talk about the brain.** Compare the brain to a path in the grass: the more it is traveled in one direction, the more visible the trail. If that trail leads to bad behaviors like drinking, drugs, or pornography, the more likely we are to stay on the path we know. Whether or not your child has looked at porn, let them know there is always a way to make a new trail!

6. **Offer hope.** If your child is using pornography, help them find healthy alternatives. If they are using it for education, let your child know you are always available to answer their questions. If they find that too embarrassing or

uncomfortable, provide them with a safe alternative like a counselor, a class you can take together, or a book. If your child is already caught in the throes of compulsive behavior, let them know there is always hope. Help your child change their behavior by praying as a family, removing or monitoring access to pornography, meeting with a counselor, giving them permission to fail, and providing other healthy outlets like sports, academics, or service. By sharing your experience (or the experiences of others), you are showing your child that what they are consuming through the media and pornography is not real. Teach them about God's biblical design for attraction and sex. One of my favorite verses about how God wants us to enjoy sex (and even nudity!) is in Proverbs and says, "A loving doe, a graceful deer—may her breasts satisfy you always, may you ever be intoxicated with her love" (Prov. 5:19 NIV).

7. **Keep the conversation going.** Nothing demonstrates how much you truly care like following up. Thank your child for spending time with you, and let them know that this conversation isn't a onetime occurrence. Make sure you communicate to your child that you are always available to answer any questions, and you won't ever judge them for what they ask. This helps to establish trust between you and your child, trust that will help move this conversation forward in the long run.

Specific Tips for Talking about Sex Trafficking

1. **Have a family meeting.** Get the whole family together if possible (and age appropriate) to discuss the idea of trafficking in general (both labor and sex). Beforehand, research

the news to find a domestic and an international story you can share with them. You can find stories at IJM.com (International Justice Mission) and childhoodlost.com (World Vision's Childhood Lost). Ask your child how and why they think children get trafficked.

2. **Make the correlation.** Talk about the cycle of supply and demand using a commonplace example, like the coffee industry. Explain how coffeehouses like Starbucks weren't as common in the past as they are now. Starbucks created a coffee and an environment that people liked so much that they were willing to pay a premium to experience it. As the company attracted more and more customers, they expanded. The consumers created an increasing demand for coffee, and Starbucks supplied it. However, this also expanded the market, allowing room for other coffee shops and even the development of in-home coffee "experiences" like Keurig. Although it might seem like comparing apples and oranges, it's not. The laws of supply and demand are as consistent with coffee as they are within the sex industry. Pornography has always existed, but the demand for it has increased as the places to access it have also increased.

3. **Talk about safety.** Even though it might be tough for both you and your child to imagine, the fact is, they are at risk. This is a great time to talk about safety online and offline. Come to an agreement with your kids about what behaviors are acceptable to keep them safe from sexual predators.

4. **Offer hope.** Sign up as a family to donate to or raise awareness for an antitrafficking organization like International Justice Mission, Compassion International, or World Vision's Childhood Lost. Research rescue organizations you can help in your city.

▶ THE BOTTOM LINE

Pornography is everywhere, and regardless of how much you protect your family from it, it will find a way into your lives. You must be proactive in communicating with your children about the dangers of pornography, even if these conversations feel embarrassing or make you uncomfortable. While every attempt should be made to safeguard your home, it's equally important to help your kids know how to process pornography when they see it. We are all created in God's image, and sex is a gift given to us to glorify him. Using pornography for our own satisfaction objectifies others and means we do not see them as the God-created human beings they are. Forming a healthy view of sex, our bodies, and others' bodies is key.

Google (or any type of search engine or social media) is the *easiest* way for someone to look up something they need to know. Become Google for your kids. When they have a question, let them know you're the first source they need to check. Acknowledge that sometimes you may not be able to supply the answer as quickly, and it may be a lot more awkward—for both you and them—but that's okay. The more you have these conversations, the more your kids will trust you and come to you with their questions, and the less awkward the conversations will be in the long run.

Google is not the source of all things bad in the world or even on the internet. What's far more damaging is failing to create a safe place within our families for our children to ask hard questions. With some effort and intention, we can remedy this problem by taking the lead in educating them about sex and the dangers of pornography.

I fully acknowledge, apologize for, and repent from my past behavior. And I am more convicted now than ever before of the global consequences of my personal actions. Please educate your children about these matters, not only for their own health and well-being but also for the health, safety, and well-being of men, women, and children all over the world.

EXPERTS WANT YOU TO KNOW

David R. Long, MD, is a graduate of the Texas Tech University School of Medicine and works as an urgent care and occupational medicine physician. After he saw the effects of addiction while working at an urgent care clinic, he became passionate about educating people about this public health issue. He speaks regularly on the disease model of addiction, hoping to improve the understanding of this affliction. He and his wife, Leigh, are parents to fourteen-year-old Samuel, thirteen-year-old Jared, and nine-year-old Lillie.

Porn addiction and *sex addiction* are terms we frequently hear in our current culture. The phrase *sexual addiction* first made an appearance in the *Diagnostic and Statistical Manual of Mental Health* in 1980 but was removed in 1994 citing a "lack of research." In the most current manual, it remains a postscript in the appendix, stating it "needs more research." Do you think compulsive use of porn (and other sexual behaviors) is an addiction just like drug, alcohol, and other classified addictions?

Sexual and chemical addictions are very similar. Brain diseases are inherently difficult to study. Couple that with the fact that funding for quality addiction studies (particularly sexual addictions) is rather scarce compared to other disease processes, and one can see why research progress would be slow.

The pathologic process that goes on deep in the midbrain of an alcoholic or heroin addict is the same as that of the gambling or sex addict. We can see it in real time with a functional MRI. With repeated exposure, that instinctual part of the brain tells the addict that this chemical or behavior is not just fun but, under stress, is absolutely necessary for survival. The midbrain lights up on MRI during drug use or even with the anticipation of drug use. The "choice" part of the brain (frontal cortex) that allows us to wisely weigh the consequences of that behavior literally gets turned off. So when we ask an addict, "How could you do that again? Didn't you think about the consequences?" The answer is no. No, they did not, and that is not a character issue. The consequences didn't even cross their mind during that craving. In fact, the consequences and shame that come as a result of the repeated behavior only serve to increase stress in the addict. That stress then pathologically triggers the midbrain to drive the addict to pursue the thing (chemical or behavioral) that it has tagged as stress relief necessary for survival. It's a devastating disease cycle.

Many people who look at pornography habitually or compulsively were first exposed innocently (unintentionally) or out of curiosity (intentionally). They want to stop and find they can't, despite their best efforts. How does this progression happen?

It is possible that the crux of all addiction treatment lies in the answer to this question. There are some who can simply put it down and walk away and others who cannot, to devastating consequences. This is not a character issue, nor is it simply a matter of will power. How do we identify who is who on this continuum? The age of exposure, frequency, and duration of exposure, as well as the intensity of the exposure all play roles in this progression. More important, the nature of the stress the person is experiencing and their coping skills (or lack thereof) are vital to predicting whether they will dabble and walk away or a behavior will become true addiction.

It is at one individual but nebulous point that a person crosses from acting on just a bad habit to having a true addiction. Therefore, the stressors our youth face today (family life, peer pressure, performance expectations) combined with a society saturated in sexuality and readily available eroticism has created a breeding ground for a cultural and spiritual crisis of epidemic proportions.

What are some of the long-term effects on children and teens who look at pornography?

Sex is supposed to be a peak of intimacy. It is not simply the mode of procreation but a deeply personal means to connect with another person. When the personal, emotional, and spiritual portions of this interaction are taken away by pornography use, we are left essentially with a drug.

When this perversion of design is introduced to a child who has no construct to work from, no sense of what "normal" is, they can develop a distorted sense of intimacy, trust, and expression of love. They are more likely to experience guilt and depression. They are more likely to engage in unhealthy relationships and have unhealthy views of sexuality. The damage from these early exposures, if not processed healthily, can cause problems well into adulthood and leave a lasting effect on marriages. This is why it is so important that we, as parents, not "live between crises." Rather than hoping this was a onetime thing or simply believing they'll grow out of it, we must seize every opportunity to discuss with our kids what they're seeing and how it affects them, taking special care to validate their feelings and give them an emotionally safe environment in which they can ask us anything and know they will be valued and respected. We must show them early what God's design for the sexual relationship should be like. They must know what normal is before they can recognize abnormal.

Does porn wire a male's brain in a different way than it wires a female's brain?

No, but the appeal and the results can be different. When we look at biology, males make about two hundred and fifty million sperm a day, where a female has one available egg per month. To successfully pass on his genes, a male is less interested in picking the best mate (as females are) and more interested in "just getting it out there."

Pornography takes away the healthy (and spiritual) relationship dynamics and intensely stimulates that primal part of the brain. That can lead to objectification of women and isolation of the individual.

Women who watch pornography can confuse the objectification they see as attention and care. That can be very appealing for a lonely girl who feels unloved or unlovable. She wants attention. She wants to be held as valuable. She wants to be cared for. If she doesn't have a healthy example of what that should look like, then these intense images can be consuming as they meet that need in a vicarious way.

This is not to say porn isn't also appealing to women in a similar manner as it is to men. The surge of dopamine and other neurochemicals can temporarily relieve stress for women just as it does for men. If they are under stress and don't have healthy stress outlets, then they can become susceptible to this repetitive behavior. The rate of women addicted to pornography is rising quickly.

What advice do you have for parents who have discovered that their child is looking at pornography? How can someone break the cycle?

We must communicate with children regularly (yeah, the really uncomfortable communication). If they feel shame about themselves, they are likely to isolate themselves, and this will push them toward true addiction. Children will have questions, and we must share our experience and knowledge about sex. We need to help them understand that their impulses are normal—even healthy—not dirty or disgusting. Parents should reinforce God's design of a healthy relationship that results in lasting happiness. Do whatever it takes to make your home free of this plague. There are great YouTube videos about how to protect your home. I would move mountains to protect my children from a bully. This is no different. Our families are constantly being assaulted by pornographic and sexualized images.

Is there a way a person's brain can be rewired from the effects of pornography use?

Once someone has seen pornographic images, they will always be there, but they can become distant and less distinct with time. The key to accomplishing this is time away from the pornography, open communication, diligent work toward developing proactive stress management strategies (e.g., a twelve-step program or counseling), and replacement of the pornography with something else. If you're married, replace it with your spouse! Make them your sole sexual outlet and see how that draws your heart (and libido!) toward them with time. A child's outlet may be sports or a hobby. Children's minds are poisoned quickly by pornography. And it can be difficult, but not impossible, to break the connection. Kids have very actively growing brains. Their brains are more moldable than adult brains and make many more connections at a much quicker pace than adult brains do. Early intervention and a safe environment in all respects is the key to success. If they can welcome pleasure and stress relief by engaging in healthy activities, then they can work their way out of this darkness. Lead them.

5

Sexually Abused Children Rarely Speak Up

How to Help

Oh, dear parent.

Please let me share something in a moment of transparency: this is the chapter I didn't want to write. I can only imagine the fear the title alone provokes as you wonder—even for a millisecond—if your child has somehow been sexually abused.

By no means does this chapter conclude or even imply that all or most children have been sexually abused. However, statistics indicate that one out of every four girls and one out of every six boys will be sexually abused by the age of eighteen. That's a minority, but it's still too many.[1]

I'm compelled to write this chapter for two reasons. First, my own story includes a history of sexual abuse. And second, the many stories I've heard from other people are evidence of how important it is to talk candidly about this issue. I don't hear these stories occasionally. I hear them *every single time* I speak at an event. If I had to estimate, that's more than 150 events over the course of eight years. These stories of sexual abuse span all ages—from eight to sixty-eight. I'm thinking, for example, of an older woman I once met at a church service. She had attended the first morning church service and afterward had hugged me and left. When I returned to my book table following the second service, she brought me a flower arrangement and a card that described how my story of abuse mirrored hers, except that her abuser was a family member.

I shared a little bit about my own sexual abuse in the early pages of this book, but because it's so relevant to this chapter, allow me to share more of that story now (legally, I've had to change a few of the insignificant details so that the perpetrator can't be identified, but the core facts of the story will never change: this person took advantage of me sexually when I was a vulnerable teenager).

When I was sixteen, I wanted to launch some ministry initiatives on my high school campus, but because my family didn't go to church for a time after my father left the ministry, I didn't have a way to connect with a youth pastor. Instead, I searched online for youth pastors who lived near the Dallas suburb where my family had recently relocated. I read a legitimate profile and, after exchanging a few emails, arranged to meet the youth pastor—a single man in his mid to late twenties who was also in Bible school—at a grocery store to get some ministry materials from him. My mom went with me, of course. She hung back a little so the youth pastor could explain some of the materials to me.

My initial attempts to launch a prayer event and Bible study at my high school failed. When the youth pastor called to follow up with me a few weeks after we met, I shared my frustration and discouragement with him and admitted I was considering leaving the faith. He encouraged me to meet him at his house so we could talk further about it.

My parents always trusted me—I was a good kid. I simply told them I was going to a friend's house to talk about church, and they didn't bat an eye. Once I arrived, it was clear the youth pastor didn't have prayer on his mind. He wanted to watch a movie with me.

At least that's what he said.

He placed blankets and pillows on his living room floor, then we went out to buy ice cream and returned to his house to watch the movie. Soon, he reached over to hold my hand. Our sexual relationship only advanced from there.

I can honestly say I don't remember much of what happened that night. Years of counseling have taught me that I've disassociated—cognitively blacked out, if you will—from most of the time he and I spent together, but I remember enough for it to have had a lasting and traumatic impact on me.

Even though I was extremely naive about what was happening at the time, I knew our relationship was sexual. And in my mind, sex was shameful and bad. I justified the situation by telling myself he wasn't *that* much older than I was, and because he was a pastor, he wouldn't do anything wrong. I also worried that if I told anyone and he got in trouble, it would leave a scandalous mark on the church.

Six months after the abuse began he told me he couldn't "see me anymore." He asked if I remembered him mentioning a female friend of his, which he had done on more than one occasion. He confessed they recently were engaged to be married, and she had no idea about our "relationship."

My heart collapsed. When he first began to abuse me, I turned to the internet for information about sex. I used pornography to help me understand what he and I were doing and then used it to ease my shame. Sex was not only associated with shame in my mind, it was also connected to love—or at least a completely inaccurate view of love that fell like wool over my innocent eyes. I had assumed he loved me because we'd had a sexual relationship.

I never mentioned it to anyone, except to tell a few friends, vaguely, that the "older guy I was dating had cheated on me and was now engaged to someone else." I didn't even define what had happened as sexual abuse until I was in my midtwenties. When the gravity of what had happened finally began to sink in, I told my counselor, "I used to say I was in a bad relationship with an older guy, but I think I might have been . . . sexually . . . abused." It was so hard to say that word. *Abused.*

As we dug into the events I remembered, my counselor confirmed that what had taken place was indeed sexual violation in every sense of the term—spiritual, emotional . . . and legal.

Over the next two years, through circumstances not of my choosing, his employer learned about his past history of sexual abuse, and he was terminated from his position in ministry. By then, I was almost twenty-eight years old and couldn't legally press charges because the statute of limitations in Texas had expired. Twelve years had passed before I was able to bring what had happened to me fully into the light.

Why Survivors of Sexual Abuse Don't Speak Up

I'm not unique. As I mentioned earlier, I've heard hundreds of stories from survivors of sexual abuse, and the young and old alike almost always share one thing in common: they keep the sexual abuse a secret. *Why?* you might wonder. Two reasons: fear and shame.

Survivors are afraid to tell. They are afraid because they think no one will believe them or that they are somehow to blame. Sadly, this fear is legitimate. When I told part of my abuse story on my blog, a very persistent commenter insisted that because I was sixteen years old at the time, I should have "known better" and therefore what had happened to me was not abuse (even though the law disagrees).

Survivors of sexual abuse are also afraid because they don't want to get someone in trouble. They transfer the responsibility from the abuser to themselves. When I had to talk to investigators about my abuse, I thought, *I don't want to break up his family or ruin his marriage. What will his wife think?*

The fact is that I am not responsible for any repercussions resulting from the violation. It was *his* decision to take advantage of me. I am not responsible for the impact that decision has had on his marriage or family life. It's taken years of therapy for me to accept and believe this truth, and some days it's still tough.

I often hear stories of sexual abuse within a family unit. Frankly, there's nothing more terrifying for a child than to think they might break up or be cast out from their own family if they reveal that a family member is sexually abusing them. The weight of this burden should not be placed on a child, but sadly, it often is.

Also, because of the particular nature of sexual abuse and our tendency to link sex with shame, survivors of sexual abuse carry a significant amount of humiliation. Often children who have been sexually abused believe they are somehow "used," "dirty," and "worthless." Saying the word *abuse* was difficult for me and happened only after a lot of time and repetition. No one wants to be a victim. What man would ever love someone who had been violated in such an intimate way? No one wants to be seen as weak or vulnerable or stupid, yet that's how many see themselves after they have been abused.

I felt shame at the thought of others speculating about the details of my abuse, and I didn't want people to think I was foolish or disingenuous. In fact, I even questioned my own intelligence at that point. I was an honors student who earned straight As and scholarship offers. Yet I believed if I was really *that* smart, I wouldn't have let this happen to me. Therefore, I concluded, I must be lacking in some mental capacity. I questioned why I didn't turn him in when I knew deep down it was wrong. Later I wondered why it took me until my twenties to understand that it was abuse. The shame and fear I felt had compelled me to keep the abuse a secret. In many ways I even kept it a secret from myself.

Some Potential Signs of Abuse

How do you know if your child is a victim of abuse? Since most children and teens won't openly admit if someone has violated them, it's imperative that parents, teachers, and responsible adults look out for warning signs.

Reflecting on my own experience, I certainly exhibited some red-flag signs. I don't blame my parents for not noticing—I was really good at hiding the signs of abuse. Since my mother and I speak freely about it now, she can, in hindsight, see how some of my behavior at the time signaled something wasn't right.

Just because a child or teenager shows one (or even a couple) of the warning signs doesn't prove they are being victimized. However, if someone is demonstrating several of these signs consistently, it definitely warrants a conversation.

A child (preadolescent) who is being (or has been) sexually abused is likely to exhibit some or all of the following behaviors:

- Experiences nightmares or other sleep problems without an explanation
- Acts distracted or distant at odd times
- Displays sudden change in eating habits: refusal to eat, a loss of appetite, or a dramatically increased appetite
- Has trouble swallowing
- Displays sudden mood swings: rage, fear, insecurity, or withdrawal
- Leaves "clues" likely to provoke a discussion about sexual issues
- Exhibits a new or unusual fear of certain people or places
- Refuses to talk about a secret shared with an adult or older child
- Writes, draws, plays, or dreams of sexual or frightening images

- Talks about a new older friend
- Suddenly has toys, money, or other gifts with no explanation
- Thinks of self or body as repulsive, dirty, or bad
- Exhibits adult-like sexual behaviors, language, and knowledge

In addition to the above behaviors, teenagers may act out by:

- Self-injuring (cutting, burning)
- Displaying inadequate personal hygiene
- Abusing drugs and/or alcohol
- Being sexually promiscuous
- Running away from home
- Becoming depressed or anxious
- Attempting suicide
- Demonstrating fear of intimacy or closeness
- Compulsively eating or dieting[2]

Trauma affects us all in different ways. Someone who is being abused may cope with their trauma in more overt ways, like acting out in anger or engaging in dangerous or self-destructive behaviors. Others process trauma internally, which can lead to depression, anxiety, and isolation.

While I was being abused, I turned inward. I began to suffer from depression and my anxiety escalated. I had nightmares and flashbacks of my abuse. I withdrew socially. My grades dropped from an A+ to a B. I missed thirty-two days of school that year (I had a friend who worked in the attendance office and covered up for me so my parents wouldn't find out).

As I entered adulthood, I began to cope in more expressive ways. I started to abuse alcohol. I became sexually involved with near-strangers. I partied with the wrong crowd. I continued to look at pornography. I struggled with an eating disorder and suicidal thoughts.

It's relatively easy to see the signs of trauma I've listed above and jump to conclusions about your own child. While this list serves as a firsthand guide, know that these signs are not the final word in determining if your child is being or has been sexually abused. Many different incidents can cause trauma in a child—a divorce or separation, a friend moving, or even a change in a school environment. We'll cover this more specifically in the Having the Conversation section at the end of this chapter to determine if you need to take additional steps in exploring this topic with your child.

The Cognitive Response to Trauma

Trauma is "stored" throughout the body: physically, emotionally, and mentally. Until it's properly addressed through counseling (especially via therapies like eye movement desensitization and reprocessing or psychosomatic experiencing, which are designed to help the body and mind process and release the trauma), it can wreak havoc on a person.

I was in my midtwenties when I first began to accept and acknowledge my sexual abuse. At the same time, I started to gain weight and suffer from extremely painful acid reflux. The reflux worsened to the point that I required daily medication and needed to have an EGD (a procedure in which a tube with a camera is inserted through the mouth and down the throat to collect images of the esophagus, stomach, and first part of the small intestines) every year to make sure I didn't have erosions or cancerous lesions. When I was almost thirty-one and had participated in tens—if not hundreds—of therapy sessions to deal with the trauma, the reflux completely cleared up. To this day, I haven't had any flare-ups. I also lost weight and have maintained a healthy weight since. Was the "stored" trauma causing my acid reflux and weight gain? I can't prove it, but I suspect there was a strong connection.

Before processing my abuse in therapy, I also regularly had nightmares. Sometimes these nightmares were sexual in nature and extremely violent. There were nights I was afraid to go to sleep because I didn't want to wake up in a panic. I underwent a sleep study at the age of twenty-six, which indicated that my brain (not my body) "woke up" more than 280 times in the course of seven hours of sleep. While I still have some sleep disturbances, I haven't had one violent nightmare or flashback since undergoing the trauma therapy.

Emotionally, at this moment, I feel fine. I don't feel anxious at all, but my body still remembers. Although I've mentally disassociated from that time, many of the memories won't go away, and I still remember some of the details. Anytime I see a car that resembles the car my abuser drove, my heart races a little bit. Whenever I pass by the places where the abuse occurred (which is fairly frequently, given my family still lives in the city where it happened), I avoid looking up. Even as I type these words, my hands are beginning to perspire and leave sweaty prints on my computer keys.

But don't let my experience confuse you. I also believe those who have experienced sexual abuse can recover from the trauma. My heart, mind, and body have recovered significantly. Healing is a continual process, and one I can't and won't give up on. While I intentionally face the facts of the situation and the knowledge that the abuse did occur, I also know that God is healing me. I believe he can and will do the same healing work in others. As Scripture says time and time again, he goes before us, he heals us, and he makes us whole (Isa. 55:9; Jer. 29:11; Rom. 8:28; Eph. 3:20).

Having the Conversation

We need to be proactive in addressing and educating our families and our churches about sexual abuse. Here are some tips to help you initiate a conversation about sexual abuse in your own home:

1. **When is the right time?** Parents frequently ask, "When's the right time to talk to my child about sexual abuse?" My response is always, "Before you think you need to." If your child is old enough to talk, they are old enough to engage in a simple conversation about anatomy and "good touch" and "bad touch" (see page 57). Always reassure your child of your unconditional love and acceptance, and create a safe space, both through your words and the environment, for them to talk.

2. **Starting the conversation.** Sometimes it's a little easier if you introduce the topic of sexual abuse by talking about a recent event you heard on the news (which sadly won't be too difficult to find), such as another child or person who was abused or mistreated. If you have experienced sexual abuse in your life and are healthy enough to talk appropriately about it, you can also initiate the conversation by talking about your own experience. Either way, speak the

truth about the situation, confirming that the person who committed the abuse was wrong in their actions, as well as the fact that the victim was not at fault. Remind your child that it's good and important that they told someone about the abuse.

3. **Ask questions.** After creating a safe place, you can move on to asking questions and making it personal. Begin asking difficult questions like, "Has someone ever showed you their private parts?" or "Has anyone ever touched your genitals?" Use whatever vocabulary your family decides is best. Let your child know that anything they tell you is okay, even if they've been sworn to secrecy.

4. **Take the right next step.** If your child has not been abused, then remind them that if anyone or anything ever makes them uncomfortable—whether that's someone touching them, showing them something in person or in a photo, or saying something inappropriate—their first step is to talk to you about it immediately.

If you learn your child might have been abused, the next step is to contact your local authorities. I know from both my own personal experience and my role as a mandatory reporter that this is a tough situation to be in. Often a person's first reaction is to deny the reality of the situation. And while this reaction is completely normal, it's not a reliable one. You might also feel compelled to talk to the abuser yourself. Although it might seem like the right thing to do before going to the authorities, in the end, both legally and personally, it is not the best choice to make. Even if you are uncertain of the abuse, the most appropriate step you can take is to bring all the information you have to the proper authorities. In most cases, you can report abuse anonymously, and if you report abuse in good faith, you are protected by the law from any legal consequences. This varies from state to state, and you can read more about reporting abuse on page 195.

▶ THE BOTTOM LINE

Fear and shame are powerful negative motivators that compel victims to keep their abuse a secret. Most abuse survivors fear what will happen when they speak up and feel deep shame for what happened to them. As a parent, you may avoid talking with your child about sexual abuse simply because you're terrified you'll learn something horrifying.

The fact is that sexual abuse causes more trauma and pain than most of us could ever possibly imagine. I chose to share this chapter of my life with the anticipation that it will help others find freedom. I want to give words to the pain survivors have experienced and hope to their hearts that God can, and will, heal them.

Be open to the growing pains healing will bring. It's not comfortable to work through traumatic experiences, and at times, the treatment can even seem more damaging than the actual abuse. Sexual abuse is never God's desire for anyone, but there is hope, a purpose, and a plan to redeem what's been lost because of it.

EXPERTS WANT YOU TO KNOW

Jimmy Fair has more than fifteen years of law enforcement experience with the US Air Force and is a corporal with the Lubbock Police Department in Lubbock, Texas. He has responded to thousands of calls involving sexual and physical abuse, child abuse and neglect, as well as the endangerment, suicides, attempted suicides, and homicides resulting from these issues. He has successfully completed diverse training offered by various expert agencies. Jimmy works alongside state agencies involved with assisting survivors of abuse and has interviewed thousands of people involved in abuse situations.

You don't have an easy job. In your opinion, why do you think so many sex crimes and abusive situations go unreported for so long? How are victims of abuse usually discovered?

Child sexual abuse crimes in particular are rarely reported for numerous reasons. Most of the crimes are committed by someone the victim knows, such as a family member or a close friend of the family. Children in general are not likely to go to the dinner table and say, "So-and-so molested me today," because it is an uncomfortable subject to bring up. Most of the time children are still learning what's right and wrong, still learning about trust in relationships, and are still a blank page to the world around them. I've also seen abuse victims not report because their abuser has threatened them with more violence if they do report.

With children, a person usually discovers the abuse accidentally. A friend or family member might see unexplained bruising or evidence of physical assault that's not consistent with the child's story. The child might say they fell down, but that wouldn't have caused the discovered trauma.

If parents suspect abuse, they should always take the child to a hospital or doctor for a checkup, as this may reveal signs of previous abuse, such as internal injuries that cannot be seen with the naked eye.

In your experience, what warning signs do those being abused exhibit?

You may observe sudden changes in a child's normal behaviors. Know your child. They may engage in drug and alcohol usage. They may block themselves off from the world. They may show symptoms of depression, including sleeping all the time, not eating, withdrawing from activities and social events, and demonstrating low self-esteem and a lack of trust in anyone. They may engage in criminal activities as a way to vent or cry out for attention. A child's resistance to spending time with a family member or friend might be a sign that the child is being abused by that person.

Physical signs of abuse range from marks and bruises to internal injuries. On small children you might see redness around or obvious injury to the genital areas or anus. Frankly, anything out of the ordinary in these areas or on the body in general warrants a visit to your physician or a local hospital. Medical professionals are trained to recognize signs of sexual and physical abuse and will know what to do. I always tell parents that it's better to be safe. If you think a child might be being abused, take action and contact somebody, even if it's just for advice.

What advice do you have for parents who learn their child is being abused?

If your child tells you they have been abused, then you need to allow them to talk. You need to ask them if they want to talk about it instead of trying to pry something out of them, as this could traumatize them further. Find out if they need immediate medical treatment and notify your local police department right away. Request an officer of the same sex to help comfort the child. Let them know they are not alone and they are very brave for telling the truth.

If they don't want to say anything at all, let them know that the suspect may be hurting and abusing other children as well, and it is important for them to come forward. They may very well save the lives of other children. Support them completely. They will probably never be the person they were before, but if they get the proper help, they will be able to heal and even grow from the experience.

Because many offenders never get caught and registered as sex offenders, it can be difficult to know how to keep our kids and families safe. What advice do you have for parents?

Speak to your child about these issues. Let them know at a young age that no one should touch their genitals or rear end, and if that happens, they should tell Mommy and Daddy. I explained this to my two boys when they were potty training, and I still tell them about people they should avoid. We can't assume kids know what's right.

We need to explain everything to our children so if they are confronted by a serious issue like sexual abuse, they'll know how to safely respond and get help. Don't shield your child from the dangers of life. Teach them about threats to their well-being, and teach them how to respond appropriately to those dangers and threats.

Know the people who spend time with your child. If someone older than your child is spending time with them, know the reason why. It is abnormal for two different age groups to hang out unless they are united by a common bond (e.g., work, friends, special organization). If someone wants to mentor your child, speak with them independently and get to know them.

Know that predators do exist, and they will target your child. Stay involved, and if you suspect something is happening, act on your suspicions.

A Note about Reporting Abuse

In the United States, mental health professionals, doctors, educators, and even sometimes clergy and others have a legal responsibility to report abuse—even if it is only suspected. These people are called mandatory reporters (I mentioned this earlier in the book). In some states, the law declares that *anyone* who, in good faith, suspects a child (or the disabled or elderly) is being abused in any way must report it to the local authorities.

The laws vary from state to state, but in most cases, reporters can be anonymous (or will be kept anonymous should any investigation progress). If a mandatory reporter suspects abuse and does not report it, and later the abuse is discovered, the reporter who did not do their due diligence can be charged with a misdemeanor or felony (again, depending on the state in which they live and in which the abuse occurred). In most circumstances, even if the suspected abuse did not occur, if the statement is made in good faith, the law protects the reporter from any charges (like defamation), which could potentially be pursued by the alleged abuser.

"Most people don't report sexual abuse because they don't want to interfere in someone else's family," says Laura Pratt, assistant city attorney and adjunct professor for the Texas Tech University School of Law. "However, your 'interference' might be the only hope of rescue a victim may have." Pratt adds that in making a report, you are not required to investigate or confront the abuser. You are simply reporting your reasonable suspicions. It is not up to you to determine whether or not your suspicions are true. A trained investigator will evaluate the child's situation.

The priority in child abuse cases is to keep a family or home intact. "The whole reason to report is to keep a child safe, and if the safest place for the child is in the home, he or she will stay there," explains Pratt. "A child abuse report itself does not mean a child will automatically be removed from the home, unless the child is in clear danger. If the environment is safe, your report can actually help to bring resources and assistance not previously available to the family and ultimately lead to healing in the family."

Often, people hesitate to report suspected abuse, which in some ways makes logical sense. If there's no solid evidence of abuse, people are concerned about the kind of consequences that could result from an erroneous report. I've heard a lot of stories and had a lot of conversations with parents and student leaders, many of whom are afraid to rock the boat when they aren't 100 percent certain abuse is taking place. It's a rational fear, but one I would like to challenge.

Hypothetically, let's say I meet a child who exhibits signs of abuse. If I determine the red flags are a genuine cause for concern, both my profession as a pastor and the state in which I live mandate that I report the suspected abuse.

Next, I'll gather as much information as I can about the child and, if possible, the suspected abuser. These are the steps I take when reporting suspected abuse, but please know that you do not have to research anything about the suspected abuser at all—you can simply report your suspicion of abuse. In most states you can make a child abuse report anonymously, and the child abuser will not find out who made the report.

After I've gathered all the information, I'll call Child Protective Services and explain what I know. At that point, my responsibility is legally over. Whether or not I choose to report anonymously, I will not find out what happens with the case unless the abuse is proven and I am needed to testify against the abuser (if I report and do not give my name, this won't happen).

Once the authorities have the information, they will determine the correct course of action. They'll research known sex offenders and possibly question the child, their parents, their peers, or their teachers. If the abuser's identity is known, they will likely question that person too.

Could this cause damage? Absolutely. Will people's feathers be ruffled, and will others be offended? Likely. Will the people involved deny the abuse, even if it's happening? Often, yes.

But let's look at the other side of the story.

Let's say the child is, in fact, being abused. If the suspected abuse is reported, investigated, and found, charges will be pressed, and the perpetrator will have to face the consequences of their actions. The abuse will stop. Healing can begin for the child, the family, and even the abuser. More often than not, the abuser has also been abused themselves.

People who damage and abuse other people need to be stopped. We must trust our law enforcement agencies and justice system to confirm or dismiss suspected abuse. But the system works only if we speak up about abuse we see or suspect.

There Is Hope

When something valuable has broken, like our great-grand-mother's vase or our favorite coffee mug, we try to fix it. We try to make it look whole again, to minimize the fine lines and cracks, to make it look, as best we can, as if it had never been broken. It's human nature to want to fix what is broken. It's also our tendency to see broken as damaged and, consciously or not, to understand never broken as equivalent to perfect.

But what if we flipped the concept of broken on its head? In essence, what if we broke the definition of broken? True, when something breaks, it no longer functions as it once did. But what if, after something breaks, it becomes *more* valuable?

Without delving too deeply into the waters of theology, let's think back to chapter 1, when we talked about ultimate and subordinate purposes. We know our ultimate purpose is to bring glory to God. But what if our subordinate purposes as human beings are a million little things, like loving others and continually seeking holiness? Might that mean that

God—knowing we are people who will mess up, fall, struggle, and mess up again—fulfills our *ultimate* purpose through his Son, Jesus, only *after* we've been broken? Perhaps God fulfills his ultimate purpose through the beauty that rises from the shards of our brokenness. And perhaps he works that way with our children too.

I first heard about the Japanese art of *kintsugi*—which literally means "to patch with gold"—from a friend. He sent me an email during a difficult time in my life, explaining how *kintsugi* artists use gold to highlight the cracks in an item when repairing it rather than trying to make a broken item look perfect again. Even when an entire piece is missing, *kintsugi* artists craft a new, custom-made piece comprised entirely of gold and designed to fit perfectly with the broken item. On its own, the broken ceramic is almost worthless; on its own, the golden replacement piece is valuable. Melded together to make one unique piece, the two separate pieces create a whole bowl that's even more valuable than before it was broken. Instead of making the broken look new, the *kintsugi* philosophy believes in restoring things to make them better than new.

This, it seems to me, is a beautiful metaphor for the restorative work Jesus does regarding our brokenness. No matter who we are, no matter our past or present circumstances, we are valuable because we are created in God's image and restored in Jesus. After a piece of us goes missing or breaks, Jesus mends us to make us whole again. We need him to cover the parts of us God can't look at because of his perfection. We crack. We break. Jesus enters and heals us, and like the *kintsugi* ceramics, we become more beautiful and more valuable than we were before.

When my friend emailed to explain what he knew about *kintsugi*, he also shared a simple prayer with me. "I pray you have peace," he wrote. "The word *shalom*, at its root in Hebrew, means 'peace.' It can be dissected further to mean 'nothing missing, nothing broken.'"

This *shalom*, this peace, is hope. This is healing.

You, your child, all of us, can have this peace through Jesus. Ephesians 2 takes the same peace described in the Old Testament, the same *shalom*, and tells us it is fulfilled and is ready for us to accept and embrace: "You lived in this world *without God* and *without hope*. But now you have been united with Christ Jesus. Once you were far away from God, but now you have been brought near to him through the blood of Christ. *For Christ himself has brought peace to us*" (Eph. 2:12–14 NLT, emphasis added).

If your heart is heavy for your child, for the challenges they may face or have already experienced, please know that this hope is available for them too. Brokenness doesn't have to be the end. Brokenness can be the beginning, the very beginning of peace. The love, mercy, and grace of Jesus is the *kintsugi* gold, a patchwork path toward hope and *shalom*, toward better than new.

It's Not Easy

I hope by now you've had a few good conversations with your kids and that this book has helped you navigate some of those discussions. And I hope it hasn't been too stressful or uncomfortable. To reiterate my intent behind this book, my aim is to educate you, encourage you to have difficult but necessary conversations with your child, and equip you with resources that will help you continue the dialogue (and the battle) over time.

I admit, writing this book was one of the most challenging endeavors of my ministry and career. I asked for extensions on my deadline *many* times because the topic continued to expand with every chapter and with every new story I heard from a parent or child. It felt like this book wasn't—and could never be—enough.

Each time I researched material for a new chapter or interviewed another expert, I felt paralyzed by the enormity of this project. The month before finishing my manuscript, I was battling laryngitis, a cold, a root canal gone wrong, holiday stress, and the weight of researching the chapters on mainstream media and pornography (in other words, heavy stuff). I laid awake for hours every night, statistics and stories running through my head. During the day, it felt like a grey veil hung over my eyes; everything in the world lost a little color and seemed tainted by evil. In a moment of honest defeat, I sat on the sofa in our living room and cried.

"I can't finish this book. The topic is just too big. It's just too much," I wept to my husband. "I feel like I'm only touching the tip of the iceberg." Tears and hiccups and gulps accompanied my fear.*

For the next fifteen minutes, Tim sat across from me and delivered a hard but necessary truth.

"You're right—it is too big. It is too much," he agreed. "And that is exactly why you are called to write it. It may be just the tip of the iceberg, but to some parents, that little tip is going to look like a mountain. Reading what you've written and beginning these conversations are their first steps into

*I'm a very ugly crier.

uncharted waters. The enemy doesn't want parents to take those steps or have those conversations. He doesn't want them to recognize what's happening so subtly in the media or how easy it is for children to access pornography. He doesn't want parents to know the warning signs of abuse or to think about how someone's personal media choices have a global impact. When you help parents who care deeply about and want to protect and teach their children about God's design for sexuality, you're interrupting Satan's plan. If these parents, their children, and one day even their grand-children—*generations*—develop a healthy view of sexuality and understand the injustices caused by our involvement in unhealthy beliefs and behaviors, it's going to set people free. Those bound by the chains of addiction and shame, those exploited and enslaved by sex trafficking will be free. The enemy wants to stop you. He's going to want to stop them. He wants this atrocious, traumatic, destructive cycle to continue, to get bigger, to suck in more people and more children."

Tim's words were encouraging, but they were also over-whelming because they illustrated the magnitude of the project.

"Remember the one?" he asked.

"The one what?"

"The one child you're writing this for."

"Yes."

Whenever my anxiety gets the best of me, and I feel over-whelmed by the sheer magnitude of what I write and speak about, I think of one person. In the case of this book, it was two people: a parent and a child. I focused my atten-tion on one parent and one child, hoping and praying that something in these pages would help to change their direction in life. What Satan has planned to use for evil, God will use for good.

It sounds impossible, but dream with me for a minute. *Maybe, just maybe . . .*

The conversations initiated as a result of this book will help deter one child from innocently Googling a word they heard at school, because they know to ask their parent instead.

Maybe this book will alert one parent to the signs of sexual abuse and allow one child to be rescued and helped.

Maybe the one person who reads this book will be the tipping point to halting the supply and demand created by the sex industry. Maybe one less woman will be trafficked, and maybe that woman will get an education and begin to help others who have been trafficked.

Maybe the cycle will end.

Helping just one person can *literally* make a world of difference. My prayer is that maybe that one person is you. Or maybe that one child is yours. Maybe your next conversation with your child is the first step in stopping the enemy in his tracks. And maybe it's you who will initiate the movement that leads to a worldwide understanding of biblical, healthy, *glorious* sexuality.

Hope from Me to You

I don't remember a lot from the years I was abused. But I do clearly recall one scene—a snapshot of me at age sixteen, curled up under a comforter on my bedroom floor. I skipped school a lot during those days. I would go home, lie on my bedroom floor, and cover myself with the sheets and the pink-and-white polka-dot comforter from my bed. I made a cocoon for myself, a place I could sleep and forget the pain I was experiencing. A place I could hide, at least temporarily.

That cocoon I made for myself is a metaphor. That's what we do when we are afraid, when we feel powerless, over-whelmed, and out of control. We bury our fears and our shame. We retreat from what scares us. Instead of reaching out, we turn inward and hide. We pull a blanket over our heads and pretend that the pain, anxiety, and brokenness don't exist.

This is exactly what I see parents doing today when it comes to the hard work of talking to their kids about sex. They try to cocoon themselves and their child from the dangers of the world. They pull that comforter around themselves and their child, hoping it will shield them from the enemy and the barrage of threats presented by the world. They hunker down in darkness and pray for the best.

Friends, let me tell you straight up: hiding does not work. Hunkering down does not work. Pulling the comforter over your head does not work. Pretending that the threats will dissipate in time does not work. I know, because none of these things worked for me. Sure, they allowed me a brief respite from the enemy's onslaught, a temporary escape. But hiding didn't solve the problem. In fact, hiding ultimately only made it worse.

What's Next?

Healing began for me the day I confided in my friend about my abuse. With that single conversation, I slowly began to peel away the comforter. Bit by bit, as I revealed more and more of my story, I stepped out of the false security of darkness and into the healing light. Conversation and communication—not hiding, not silence—were the key.

Parents, you hold that key right now. You have a choice. You can hide under the comforter and live in darkness, silence, and fear. Or you can unlock the door to hope.

Our world is broken and has been since the time of Adam and Eve and the fall. Our world is full of evil. All of us—children *and* adults—are threatened daily by the enemy. These threats take myriad forms, including many we have identified in this book: mainstream media, pornography, sex trafficking, sexual abuse.

But . . .

Hope exists. Peace is possible. You, as a parent, have the power to halt the enemy's insidious work. Reading this book might be your first step. But I urge you to continue to arm yourself with the knowledge, information, and resources that will help you continue to protect your children. Above all, talk to your children continually. Get creative in the ways you approach them and initiate dialogue. Be open and nonjudgmental. Be the person they can trust.

And know, too, that you are not alone on this journey. God—Immanuel—is with you every step of the way. You have a God who sustains you with his strength, envelops you in his love, and surrounds you as your shield:

> You, O LORD, you are a shield around me;
>> you are my glory, the one who holds my head
>>> high.
> I cried out to the LORD,
>> and he answered me from his holy mountain.

I lay down and slept,
    yet I woke up in safety,
    for the LORD was watching over me.
I am not afraid of ten thousand enemies
    who surround me on every side.

                      Psalm 3:3–6 NLT

I pray that you, your family now, and your family that is to come will know hope and freedom. I pray that as you and I and the world mend from this assault and are restored, the brightness of Christ will illuminate our broken places with his beautiful healing power.

I'd like to close this book with a few words from my close friend Carly, whom I mentioned in chapter 4. She was a "good girl" who was sexually abused and turned to the internet for answers, much like me. If you're still wondering whether having these conversations with your child is the right thing for you to do, read Carly's words now, as a twenty-two-year-old:

> Eight years ago, as a fourteen-year-old girl, I wouldn't have wanted my mother or father to sit me down to have "the talk" about sex and pornography. No teenager really wants to have that talk. It's uncomfortable for both parties.
>
> But looking back on my childhood and teenage years, I wish my parents had spoken to me about these things. I truly think the way you approach your child makes all the difference. You can show love and a concern for them, or you can be bold and blunt. No child is going to like a strict list of things they can and cannot do—they'll just want to rebel and break the rules. But approaching them with a sincere heart and sharing how much you care about them and their well-being could positively influence their behavior. My parents

never had the talk with me, but I think if they would have, it would have saved me years of hurt.

My final encouragement to you is that it is *never* too late to talk to your child about porn or sex. If you haven't yet, don't feel like a failure. Even if it's uncomfortable, it's the right thing to do. Pray about talking to them, keeping in mind that nothing is impossible with Christ. And don't forget that God is with you every step of the way!

You have been presented with a lot of information, statistics, and stories in this book. Some of this may be disheartening and some may be encouraging. Some may be shocking and some may be hopeful. Regardless, I hope you see that *you are essential to your child's spiritual and sexual development.* God has uniquely gifted you to lead, to parent, to guide, to encourage, and to equip those in your care. Yes, the world is broken, but it is not hopeless. You have the tools (and hopefully the courage) to influence your child's life. You can change the way your child interprets and responds to this world's distorted view of sexuality. It's now up to you to embrace this responsibility and equip your child to understand the wonderful gift of sex God has given us.

Are you ready?

Love your children.

Lead your children.

I said it in the beginning of this book, and I will reiterate it now at the end: *let's redeem the conversation.*

Resources for the Conversation

This may be the first chapter you turn to. I understand. You have a pressing question, and you don't want any fluff. Let's tear the bandage off as quickly as possible and avoid any unnecessary awkwardness.

This *is* your book. I'm not going to tell you how to read it. But may I suggest that you scan some of the other chapters? These resources are helpful, in and of themselves, but to have successful, ongoing conversations about sex with your family, you need to understand the big picture. Behavioral changes can always be made. Technology filters can be applied. Ground rules can be set. You can change your actions, but unless you base them on a biblical and healthy view of sexuality, you won't change your heart.

Because technology is always changing, I'm a little leery that between the time I write this book and the time you read it, the landscape will have changed dramatically. I'll do my best to keep 5ThingsBook.com updated with new articles, information, research, and resources. And it's my hope that

I'll be able to update the statistics and information contained in the book every time it's reprinted.

The following resources have been organized by chapters in 5 *Things Every Parent Needs to Know about Their Kids and Sex.*

Introduction: Sex Is a Gift from God

Additional Reading

- *God Loves Sex: An Honest Conversation about Sexual Desire and Holiness* by Drs. Dan Allender and Tremper Longman III
- *The Mingling of Souls: God's Design for Love, Marriage, Sex, and Redemption* by Matt Chandler
- *Sacred Marriage: What If God Designed Marriage to Make Us Holy More Than to Make Us Happy* by Gary Thomas
- *The Truth about Sex: What the World Won't Tell You and God Wants You to Know* by Kay Arthur

Chapter 1: The Earlier, the Better

Additional Reading

- *A Chicken's Guide to Talking Turkey with Your Kids about Sex* by Dr. Kevin Leman and Kathy Flores Bell
- *The Focus on the Family® Guide to Talking with Your Kids about Sex* by The Physicians Resource Council

- *Hooked: New Science on How Casual Sex Is Affecting Our Children* by Drs. Joe S. McIlhaney Jr. and Freda McKissic Bush
- *How and When to Tell Your Kids about Sex: A Lifelong Approach to Shaping Your Child's Sexual Character (God's Design for Sex)* by Stan and Brenda Jones
- *The Talk: 7 Lessons to Introduce Your Child to Biblical Sexuality* by Luke Gilkerson

Especially for Girls

- *And the Bride Wore White: Seven Secrets to Sexual Purity* by Dannah Gresh
- *Five Conversations You Must Have with Your Daughter* by Vicki Courtney
- *The Girl's Body Book: Everything You Need to Know for Growing Up YOU* by Kelli Danham
- *Raising a Lady in Waiting: Parent's Guide to Helping Your Daughter Avoid a Bozo* by Jackie Kendall
- *Six Ways to Keep the "Little" in Your Girl: Guiding Your Daughter from Her Tweens to Her Teens* by Dannah Gresh

Especially for Boys

- *The Boy's Body Book: Everything You Need to Know for Growing Up YOU* by Kelli Dunham
- *Conversations You Must Have with Your Son* by Vicky Courtney

- *Six Ways to Keep the "Good" in Your Boy: Guiding Your Son from His Tweens to His Teens* by Dannah Gresh

Additional Resources for Parents of LGBTQ Teens

- *Love Is an Orientation: Elevating the Conversation with the Gay Community* by Andrew Marin
- *Torn: Rescuing the Gospel from the Gays-vs.-Christians Debate* by Justin Lee
- *Washed and Waiting* by Wesley Hill

Websites

- Freed Hearts: For Parents, Our Gay Kids, and the Church: patheos.com/blogs/freedhearts
- Gay Christian Network Forum: gaychristian.net
- Unconditional Ministries: beunconditional.org

Chapter 2: Your Child Is Not the Exception

Additional Reading

- *Fallen: Out of the Sex Industry and into the Arms of the Savior* by Annie Lobert
- *Inside of Me: Lessons of Lust, Love and Redemption* by Shellie R. Warren
- *The Reason: How I Discovered a Life Worth Living* by Lacey Sturm

Chapter 3: Kids Consume Sexual Messages through Mainstream Media

Additional Reading

- *Growing Up Social: Raising Relational Kids in a Screen-Driven World* by Gary Chapman and Arlene Pellicane
- *Parenting for the Digital Age: The Truth Behind Media's Effect on Children and What to Do about It* by Bill Ratner
- *Plugged-In Parenting: How to Raise Media-Savvy Kids with Love, Not War* by Bob Waliszewski
- *A Practical Guide to Parenting in the Digital Age: How to Nurture Safe, Balanced, and Connected Children and Teens* by Dr. Winifred Lloyds Lender
- *Touchy Subjects: Talking to Kids about Sex, Tech, and Social Media in a Touchscreen World* by Craig Gross with David Dean

Chapter 4: Google Is the New Sex Ed

Additional Reading: Pornography

- *Good Pictures Bad Pictures: Porn-Proofing Today's Young Kids* by Kristen Jenson with Dr. Gail Poyner
- *Pornland: How Porn Has Hijacked Our Sexuality* by Gail Dines*
- *Porn Nation: Conquering America's #1 Addiction* by Michael Leahy
- *Truth Behind the Fantasy of Porn: The Greatest Illusion on Earth* by Dr. Shelley Lubben
- *Wired for Intimacy: How Pornography Hijacks the Male Brain* by Dr. William Struthers

* Read with caution.

Additional Reading for Adults Struggling with Pornography and/or Compulsive Sexual Behaviors

- *A Christian Woman's Guide to Breaking Free from Pornography: It's Not Just a Guy's Problem* by Shelley Hitz and S'ambrosia Curtis
- *Delivered—True Stories of Men and Women Who Turned from Porn to Purity* by Matt Frau
- *Dirty Girls Come Clean* by Crystal Renaud
- *Every Man's Battle: Winning the War on Sexual Temptation One Victory at a Time* by Stephen Arterburn
- *Every Woman's Battle: Discovering God's Plan for Sexual and Emotional Fulfillment* by Shannon Ethridge and Stephen Arterburn
- *No Stones: Women Redeemed from Sexual Addiction* by Marnie Ferree
- *Shattered Vows: Hope and Healing for Women Who Have Been Sexually Betrayed* by Debra Laaser
- *Surfing for God: Discovering the Divine Desire Beneath Sexual Struggle* by Michael John Cusick

Additional Reading about Sex Trafficking

- *Not for Sale: The Return of the Global Slave Trade—and How We Can Fight It* by David Batstone
- *The White Umbrella: Walking with Survivors of Sex Trafficking* by Mary Frances Bowley

Websites

- Childhood Lost (World Vision): childhoodlost.com
- Compassion International: compassion.com

- Covenant Eyes Internet Accountability and Filtering: covenanteyes.com
- Fight the New Drug: fightthenewdrug.com
- International Justice Mission: IJM.com
- XXX Church: XXXchurch.com

Chapter 5: Sexually Abused Children Rarely Speak Up

Additional Reading

- *Helping Your Child Recover from Sexual Abuse* by Caren Adam and Jennifer Fay
- *Hush: Moving from Silence to Healing after Childhood Sexual Abuse* by Nicole Braddock Bromley
- *Not Marked: Finding Hope and Healing after Sexual Abuse* by Mary DeMuth
- *On the Threshold of Hope* by Dr. Diane Langberg
- *Victims No Longer: The Classic Guide for Men Recovering from Sexual Child Abuse* by Mike Lew
- *The Wounded Heart: Hope for Adult Victims of Childhood Sexual Abuse* by Dr. Dan Allender

Websites

- Childhelp USA (National Child Abuse Hotline): 1.800.4.A.CHILD; childhelp.org
- Child Welfare Information Gateway: childwelfare.gov
- National Center for Missing and Exploited Children: missingkids.com/home
- National Center for Victims of Crime: victimsofcrime.org
- National Children's Advocacy Center: nationalcac.org

- National Sexual Violence Resource Center: nsvrc.org
- Network of Victim Assistance: novabucks.org
- Rape, Abuse & Incest National Network: rainn.org

Apps and Other Resources

Smartphone App Guide

Ask.fm

Intended Purpose:
- Allows users to ask questions and answer those posted by other users while remaining anonymous.
- Posts can automatically post to Facebook and other social media accounts.

Potential Dangers:
- Bullying is the main concern with this app, as users ask derogatory questions about specific peers and other peers are encouraged to respond.

App Rating:
- 12+

Blendr

Intended Purpose:
- Allows users to send messages, photos, videos, and even rate the hotness of other users within the geographical location of the user.

Potential Dangers:
- This app is intended for the purpose of flirting and meeting up with other users.
- There are no authentication requirements, so minors can easily be contacted by adults and vice versa.

App Rating:
- 17+

Down (formerly Bang with Friends)

Intended Purpose:
- Allows users to rate individuals for the prospect of just hanging out or if they are "down" for a sexual hookup.
- Prospective connections are limited to Facebook friends.
- When two users indicate they are down, each user is notified and encouraged to contact the other.

Potential Dangers:
- Creates a hookup norm within a peer group.

App Rating:
- 17+

Dubsmash

Intended Purpose:
- Users choose their favorite sound or movie quote, record themselves with the sound, and then share the video with friends or post to a public space.

Potential Dangers:

- Videos can depict explicit imagery and language.
- User-submitted sounds can be sexual, violent, explicit, or racist/hateful.

App Rating:

- 12+

Facebook

Intended Purpose:

- Users connect online with friends, family, and colleagues by posting status updates, pictures, videos, and more.
- Users can enable privacy settings on their account to hide their content from strangers. When enabled, new "friends" have to be accepted to view their content.

Potential Dangers:

- Users can selectively hide content from specific users (e.g., parents).
- Users can easily post something private by accident.
- Users can receive friend requests and private messages from all other members unless privacy settings are enabled.
- Users can be found by searching by name or email address unless privacy settings are enabled.

Age Limit:

- 13+

Instagram

Intended Purpose:

- Users can view and post photos and videos for friends and family to "like" and comment on.
- Different filtering options allow the user to customize their content.
- Users can enable privacy settings on their account to hide their content from strangers. When enabled, new followers have to be approved to view their content.

Potential Dangers:

- All users have access to the "popular" section and have the ability to search for other users and keywords. Search history can be cleared with a push of a button.
- Explicit content is accessible to any user who explores the popular section and by following accounts of people they do not know.
- Posts can show a user's exact location if location services are enabled.

App Rating:

- 12+

Kik Messenger

Intended Purpose:

- As a private messaging service, users can send photos, videos, sketches, and memes to other Kik users.
- Users can only contact other users if they know their username.

Potential Dangers:

- Often used as a texting alternative to hide conversations from parents or other adults, which poses a sexting concern.
- Friend requests can be sent by strangers if usernames become public, and adult predators can easily pose as teens and/or peers to connect with minors.
- Chat rooms in Kik are easily accessed and contain explicit content.

App Rating:

- 17+

Musical.ly

Intended Purpose:

- Users create videos lip-synching to popular music and share with friends.

Potential Dangers:

- Can use any song. Videos can be shared and downloaded to personal devices. Songs include sexually explicit or violent content.

App Rating:

- 12+

Omegle

Intended Purpose:

- Encourages users to make new friends by choosing another user at random to have a one-on-one video chat.

- Chat participants are identified only as "You" and "Stranger."

Potential Dangers:

- This app's tagline is "talk to strangers" because you don't know who will be on the other end of the chat.
- This is a prime atmosphere for adult predators to interact with minors to get personal information or expose themselves.
- The app is full of graphic nudity supplied by users.

App Rating:

- 13+

Periscope

Intended Purpose:

- Live stream video to anyone, anywhere, from your mobile phone.

Potential Dangers:

- Videos can contain images and captions containing rude humor, sexually suggestive material, and offensive behavior. Recommended videos may also contain pornography or explicit or vulgar behavior. A chat feature allows other users to engage in the video creator. And with an age setting of four years old and older, the potential for child predators and exploitation is huge.

App Rating:

- 4+

Poof

Intended Purpose:

- Allows users to select which apps on smartphones and tablets they wish to hide, and the icons will no longer appear on the screen.
- Device has to be "jailbroken" for this app to work.

Potential Dangers:

- Gives the user the ability to hide restricted, dangerous, and explicit apps from parents' view.

App Rating:

- 4+

Snapchat

Intended Purpose:

- Allows users to receive and send photos to friends that once opened by the recipient will disappear within ten seconds (the sender chooses how long the image will appear).
- Privacy settings are available to prevent receiving content from strangers.

Potential Dangers:

- Due to the time limitations of sent content, this app has become the go-to app for sexting among teens.
- The recipient can save content by taking a screenshot to send to others. Additional apps like Snap-Hack have been created to give recipients the ability to save pictures that are sent to them in Snapchat.

App Rating:

- 12+

Tinder

Intended Purpose:

- Allows users to rate other profiles based on their pictures for the prospect of dating or sexual hookup by swiping right to like and left to not like.
- Members are limited to those with a Facebook account. Content from Facebook, such as pictures, interests, and more, is loaded into the app.
- Potential connections are limited to a user-specified location.
- When two users are a match (both swiped to like), they are notified and encouraged to private message one another.

Potential Dangers:

- Tinder is designed for adult use and is limited to those whose Facebook accounts indicate they are eighteen years or older.
- Minors (who fake their age on Facebook to gain access) using this app are brought into immediate contact with adults.

App Rating:

- 17+

Twitter

Intended Purpose:

- Twitter is used to communicate online in posts of 140 characters or less called Tweets.
- Users can enable privacy settings on their account to hide their content from strangers. When enabled, new followers have to be approved to view their content.

Potential Dangers:

- Spam bots are notorious for following users as a way to receive more followers in return. These accounts can contain explicit content, as Twitter does not block explicit material.
- Users can receive private messages from anyone they allow to follow them.
- Users can also send private messages to anyone who follows them.
- If an account isn't private, anyone can view and/or redistribute their content.

Age Limit:

- 13+

Vine

Intended Purpose:

- Users can view and post videos that are limited to six seconds and continually loop.

- Users can enable privacy settings on their account to hide their content from strangers. When enabled, new followers have to be approved to view their content.

Potential Dangers:
- Explicit content is easily accessible, including nudity, language, and violence.
- Users are dared by peers to try dangerous things for high ratings and popularity.
- Videos are public by default and privacy settings must be enabled to limit visibility.

App Rating:
- 17+

 Whisper

Intended Purpose:
- Allows users to place text over a picture to share their thoughts and feelings anonymously.

Potential Dangers:
- Even though it is anonymous, the geographical location of the user is displayed and users can search for users close by.
- Due to the geographical component to this app, it is also a meeting app where online relationships are encouraged.
- In 2013, a man in Seattle was charged with raping a twelve-year-old girl he met on Whisper.[1]

App Rating:
- 17+

Yik Yak

Intended Purpose:
- Allows users to send text-only posts to an anonymous social wall.
- Posts can be up to two hundred characters in length and viewable to up to five hundred users in the poster's geographical location.

Potential Dangers:
- No username or password is required, which allows the user to remain anonymous.
- Users can be exposed to content of an abusive and even sexual nature and has been used as a form of cyber-bullying.

App Rating:
- 17+

9GAG

Intended Purpose:
- Allows users to upload images with captions and text (memes).
- Users sign up using their Facebook or Google+ accounts or with an email address.

Potential Dangers:
- No moderation. Posts can contain images and captions containing rude humor, sexually suggestive material, and offensive behavior.

- Users can easily choose a NSFW (not safe for work) category, which exposes them to nudity, sexual refrences, and vulgar language.

App Rating:
- 12+

Online Monitoring and Filter Programs

covenanteyes.com

XXXchurch.com

netnanny.com

Basic Parental Controls

Please note that these links were valid at the time of publication but, depending on when you read this book, may no longer be active. For the most current links to parental controls on popular devices, please visit 5ThingsBook.com. And most important, don't let turning on parental controls take the place of a conversation with your child.

Apple

For instructions on how to use parental controls for Apple computers, visit: https://support.apple.com/kb/PH18571?loc ale=en_US (if the link does not work, simply conduct a web search for "parental controls for Apple computers" for the most recent information).

For instructions on how to use parental controls for iPods, iPads, and iPhones, visit: https://support.apple.com/en-us /HT201304 (if the link does not work, simply conduct a web search for "parental controls for iPods, iPads, or iPhones" for the most recent information).

Author recommendation: My husband and I both installed Covenant Eyes on our computers, iPhones, and iPads, have disabled Safari, and use the Covenant Eyes browser. On Apple products, the "restrictions" can be a parent's best friend for putting technological barriers in the way of easy access to pornography.

Windows

Windows makes it fairly simple for a parent to set up controls, including what times someone can use the computer. For more instructions, visit http://windows.microsoft.com/en-us/windows/set-parental-controls#1TC=windows-7.

Android Phones and Tablets

For any Android-based phone or tablet (almost anything that is not Apple), you can find device and app parental controls in the Google Play support section: https://support.google.com/googleplay/answer/1075738?hl=en.

Amazon Kindle

Like Amazon Prime, Amazon Kindle also requires a PIN to access restrictions. Visit http://www.amazon.com/gp/help/customer/display.html?nodeId=201242840.

Smart TVs

You no longer need a smart Blu-ray player. Most new TVs are internet capable with web browsing and a variety of apps like Netflix and Hulu. To find certain parental controls for your specific TV, do a web search for the brand and model of your TV (i.e., "Samsung UN40J6200 parental controls"), or consult your user manual for instructions.

YouTube

- Put the YouTube app for kids on your device and deactivate the standard YouTube app.
- Turn on "Restricted Mode" for YouTube viewing online (it's currently located at the bottom of the page). If you have a Google or YouTube account, you can log in and lock this mode so even when you're signed out, anyone who uses YouTube from that browser will have restrictions turned on.

Xbox One

Xbox has continued to improve safety features for families. For the most recent guide on setting parental controls and safety information, visit http://support.xbox.com/en-US/xbox -one/security/core-family-safety-features.

PlayStation

PlayStation doesn't make their parental controls exceptionally easy to find online, and their links change rapidly. It took me a little while to find the manual for the PS3 parental controls, which can be found online here: http://manuals. playstation.net/document/en/ps3/current/basicoperations/ parentallock.html. I recommend you look at the user manual before searching online as it may be easier. I'll do my best to keep 5ThingsBook.com updated with the latest links as well.

Nintendo

Parental controls for all Nintendo devices include the ability to limit the time a user can engage in play, as well as internet blocking. Included in this list are the Nintendo Wii and DS systems: http://en-americas-support.nintendo.com/app /answers/detail/a_id/10530/p/604.

Parental Controls for Netflix

It's easy to set parental controls for Netflix; however, you must be vigilant and know that if your child logs in as someone other than their username or watches Netflix at a friend's house, then access to unrated, pornographic movies is readily available with no safeguards. Visit https://help.netflix.com/en /node/264.

Amazon Prime

I find Amazon Prime's parental controls pretty helpful as they use a PIN to control restrictions regardless of the login. Visit http://www.amazon.com/gp/help/customer/display.html ?nodeId=201423060.

VUDU

VUDU, a popular movie rental app (think Redbox but at home!), doesn't have a robust parental control formula. Currently, you can filter by MPAA rating and online playback has no parental controls. Visit http://vudu.custhelp.com/app/answers /detail/a_id/48/~/does-vudu-have-parental-controls%3F.

Acknowledgments

There are many people in my life to whom I owe a great debt of gratitude. My friends and family: a thank-you is not enough for the seasons of life you have lived with me. (Especially you, Amy. Especially you.)

To Tim, my husband and my favorite: thank you for loving me authentically and fully known. This book would not exist if it weren't for you encouraging me along the way to write it, even during the million times I wanted to quit. Thank you for choosing me, praying for and with me, and being the most godly man I know.

To those who helped with their expertise and talent to make this book its best, I'm indebted to your professionalism, graciousness, and commitment to excellence. Tara Shepherd Brown, Bryan Norman, Chad Allen, Michelle DeRusha, Amy McKenzie, Amy Ballor, Jim Chaffee, Brian Smith, Adam Edelstein, Emily Davis, Lexie Florence, and all my expert contributors who so freely gave their time and talent.

To my readers, thank you. Your support, input, and encouragement as I've written this book provided me with more honest stories and personal insights than I could have ever experienced alone. I pray this book is as much a blessing to you as you have been to me.

There are many people I adore all over the country. To those in California, Texas, Tennessee, Michigan, and Iowa—I can't tell you how much your support carries me.

And, of course, I am forever grateful to my Savior who knew my sin and shame and wore it nailed to a cross. You carried my weight so I didn't have to. You are my hope, and you are the hope of every man, woman, and child who will ever breathe the air in this glorious world you created.

Notes

Author's Note

1. Although I have hundreds of hours of pastoral counseling as a minister under my belt and have completed some formal training and education in family sociology and sexual trauma in adolescents, I am not a doctor or licensed counselor. Please do not interpret this book as medical or psychiatric advice. At the time of this book's publication, I am in the process of continuing my education with an integrated focus in psychology, specializing in research in the areas of trauma and addiction. I am also taking seminary-level courses in theology and ministry. I've included professional insights from highly respected licensed clinicians, doctors, and attorneys, as well as licensed therapists who focus on family, adolescent sexuality, and addiction. I am grateful for their words of wisdom and guidance during the process of researching and writing this book.

Preface

1. Did you know pornography and sex addiction are not clinically classified as addictions? Clinicians use the *Diagnostic and Statistical Manual of Mental Disorders* (DSM) to diagnose mental disorders and addictions. The most recent manual, the DSM-V, was published in 2013. In earlier DSMs, hypersexuality disorder (HD) was coined to help clinicians diagnose people with symptoms. But in 1994, the diagnosis was revoked and now remains a postscript in the appendix stating it "needs more research." There are many opinions on what classifies HD, but most include increased frequency and intensity of sexually motivated arousal and urges and behaviors lasting longer than six months. Since pornography addiction is not a clinically recognized term, I won't use it. I will term my behavior, and other similar behaviors, as "compulsive behaviors." However, I believe there is enough evidence to prove sexually based addictions. Like alcoholism or drug

addiction, increasing and compulsive use of pornography or other sexual behaviors that interfere with a functional daily life should be considered an addiction (and I hope someday will be so that treatment options will be more accessible for those who suffer).

2. Hearing other people open up about their encounters with broken sexuality has become an everyday occurrence for me. To keep myself healthy, I've put systems in place in my own life, such as professional counseling, support from my friends and the church, and encouragement from my husband. These systems help me carry the weight of the dark and heavy stories I hear. It's emotionally hard work, but I am able to keep moving forward with my head held high and my heart open, ready to give and receive.

Introduction

1. I owe a great deal of gratitude to Denny Burk and Dr. Tim Alan Gardner for their extensive research and pursuit of a better understanding of a theology of sex. Their books (respectively) *What Is the Meaning of Sex?* and *Sacred Sex: A Spiritual Celebration of Oneness in Marriage* helped me in my research and writing about what "the gift of sex" really means. I highly recommend both books if you would like a more robust understanding of what the Bible says about sexuality.

2. Genesis 1:21, 22, 24.

3. Genesis 2:21–22.

4. One of the many therapies that helped me is called eye movement desensitization and reprocessing (EMDR), which is known for its effect on post-traumatic stress disorder. I also benefited from another kind of therapy that works on releasing the psychosomatic (mind/body) symptoms many abuse survivors experience.

5. Amy Shaffner, "What 'True Love Waits' Didn't Prepare Me For," Marriage Roots, April 8, 2015, http://www.marriageroots.com/what-true-love-waits-didnt -prepare-me-for/. My neighbor Amy is seriously the best wife and mom out there because she is honest. You should read more of what she writes on this website.

Chapter 1 The Earlier, the Better

1. Thomas J. Fitch, MD and David Davis, ed., *The Focus on the Family® Guide to Talking with Your Kids about Sex* (Grand Rapids: Revell, 2005, 2013), 131.

2. Ibid., 69.

3. Ibid., 87.

4. Ibid., 109.

5. Ibid., 131.

6. Casey E. Copen, PhD, Anjani Chandra, PhD, and Gladys Martinez, PhD, "Prevalence and Timing of Oral Sex with Opposite-Sex Partners among Females and Males Aged 15–24 Years: United States, 2007–2010," *National Health Statistics Report*, no. 56 (August 16, 2012): 1, http://www.cdc.gov/nchs/data/nhsr/ nhsr056.pdf.

7. Ibid., 2.

8. Anne Marie Tiernon, "Oral Sex Survey," wthr.com, accessed January 2015, http://www.wthr.com/story/4560345/oral-sex-survey.

9. Meredith O'Brien, "Wrong Messages: Young Kids Are Casually Experimenting with Oral Sex," Dr. Sharon Maxwell, accessed January 2015, http://www.drsharonmaxwell.com/articles_other_wrongmessages.html.

10. Claire McCarthy, "Sorry Parents, 'The Talk' Just Got Harder," *Thriving* (blog), November 9, 2010, http://childrenshospitalblog.org/sorry-parents-the-talk-just-got-harder.

11. There's probably a philosophy out there that says, "It's not normal and not acceptable," but that goes against the belief that God created us to experience sexual pleasure, so we're not going to consider the idea that masturbation is "not normal" because I think the idea is unscriptural.

12. Geoff Ashley, "Is Masturbation Sinful?," The Village Church, December 14, 1010, www.thevillagechurch.net/sermon/is-masturbation-sinful/.

13. Resnick, Bearman, and Blum, et al., "Protecting Adolescents from Harm," *Journal of the American Medical Association*, 278, no. 10 (September 10, 1997): 823–32, http://www.ncbi.nlm.nih.gov/pubmed/9293990.

14. Fitch and Davis, *The Focus on the Family® Guide*, 153.

15. Ibid.

16. Dr. R. Albert Mohler Jr., "Sexual Orientation and the Gospel of Jesus Christ," albertmohler.com, November 13, 2014, http://www.albertmohler.com/2014/11/13/sexual-orientation-and-the-gospel-of-jesus-christ/.

17. Thank you, pastor. You know who you are.

Chapter 2 Your Child Is Not the Exception

1. Comments taken and modified from: http://www.annemariemiller.com/2013/08/19/three-things-you-dont-know-about-your-children-and-sex/, last accessed June 27, 2015.

2. Jen Sandbulte, "Wakeup Call," *Jen Sandbulte—Real Christianity, Real Life* (blog), April 8, 2015, http://jensandbulte.com/wakeup-call/.

Chapter 3 Kids Consume Sexual Messages through Mainstream Media

1. James P. Steyer, *The Other Parent: The Inside Story of Media's Effect on Our Children* (New York: Atria Books, 2003), 4.

2. Victor C. Strasburger, Barbara J. Wilson, and Amy B. Jordan, *Children, Adolescents, and the Media* (New York: Sage Publications, 2014), 231–32.

3. Ibid., 233.

4. Strasburger, Wilson, and Jordan, *Children, Adolescents, and the Media*.

5. Ibid., 16.

6. Ibid., 201.

7. As I researched more about ABC Family, in December 2014, the network announced it was going to offer a new transgendered-focused docuseries, *My Transparent Life*, which follows a boy whose parents recently divorced and whose father is in the process of becoming a woman. "ABC Family is best known for its complex, loving, and relatable family programming," said ABC Family president Tom Ascheim. While part of me thinks it's progressive and brave to speak about

topics usually swept under the rug, I am concerned about the way the show is being marketed to impressionable young minds.

8. Rebecca Brayton, "Top 10 TV Shows You Shouldn't Watch with Your Parents," Watch Mojo, accessed August 24, 2015, http://www.watchmojo.com/video/id/12298/. Watch with discretion.

9. MPAA (movie) ratings are surprisingly stricter than the NR or MA ratings on network TV and don't have theater staff to monitor who is watching. These are the uncut versions on TV, while theatrical is cut/rated to MPAA (R, PG13, etc.).

10. Strasburger, Wilson, and Jordan, *Children, Adolescents, and the Media*, 211.

11. Anith Busch, "*Wolf of Wall Street* Had Its Own Consigliere for R-Rating in Tom Sherak; Exhibs Waiting to See How It Plays in Peoria," Deadline, December 16, 2013, http://deadline.com/2013/12/wolf-of-wall-street-ratings-behind-the-scenes-653213/.

12. Strasburger, Wilson, and Jordan, *Children, Adolescents, and the Media*, 214.

13. Hope Schreiber, "A History of Weird Sexual Innuendo in Children's Movies," Complex, January 14, 2014, http://www.complex.com/pop-culture/2014/01/sexual-innuendo-childrens-movies/the-rescuers.

14. Max Pearl, "Meet the Man Behind Lil Jon & DJ Snake's 'Turn Down for What' Video," Thump, March 20, 2014, http://thump.vice.com/words/the-daniels-turn-down-for-what-directors-interview.

15. Ibid., 219.

16. Ibid., 219.

17. Ibid., 461.

18. Ibid., adapted from information presented on www.esrb.org.

19. "Rating Information: *Story of Seasons*," Entertainment Software Rating Board, last accessed August 24, 2015, http://www.esrb.org/ratings/synopsis.jsp?Certificate=33785&Title=STORY%20OF%20SEASONS&searchkeyword.

20. "Rating Information: *Etrian Mystery Dungeon*," Entertainment Software Rating Board, last accessed August 25, 2015, http://www.esrb.org/ratings/synopsis.jsp?Certificate=33764&Title=Etrian%20Mystery%20Dungeon&searchkeyword.

21. "Rating Information: *Dark Souls*," Entertainment Software Rating Board, accessed August 25, 2015, http://www.esrb.org/ratings/synopsis.jsp?Certificate=33866&Title=Dark%20Souls%20II%3A%20Scholar%20of%20the%20First%20Sin&searchkeyword.

22. "Rating Information: *Omega Quintet*," Entertainment Software Rating Board, accessed August 25, 2015, http://www.esrb.org/ratings/synopsis.jsp?Certificate=33830&Title=Omega%20Quintet&searchkeyword.

23. "Rating Information: *Grand Theft Auto V*," Entertainment Software Rating Board, accessed August 25, 2015, http://www.esrb.org/ratings/synopsis.jsp?Certificate=33755&Title=Grand%20Theft%20Auto%20V&searchkeyword=grand%20theft%20auto.

Chapter 4 Google Is the New Sex Ed

1. Ashlyn Tubbs, "Frenship High School Increases Security after Gun Threat on App," *KCBD*, December 9, 2014, http://www.kcbd.com/story/27587349/frenship-high-school-increases-security-after-gun-threat-on-app.

2. It released in the United Kingdom in 1965.

3. *Forbes*, March 1, 1971, 19; *Business Week*, August 9, 1969, 98; *Time*, November 7, 1969, 88, as cited in Gail Dines, *Pornland: How Porn Has Hijacked Our Sexuality* (Boston: Beacon Press, 2011), 13. It is difficult for me to recommend this book due to the nature of its X-rated language, however, I think it's important for us to understand the extreme forms of pornography that are readily available and accessible to our children, teens, and even to us as adults. It is not a read for the sensitive spirits, and I even needed to skip a few pages because of how explicit some of her research findings are.

4. Larry Flynt, *Hustler*, 1974, 9, as cited in Dines, *Pornland*, 15.

5. Ibid. Flynt used an explicit phrase that I replaced here.

6. Dines, *Pornland*, xvii.

7. Ibid., 13.

8. US Department of Justice, Post Hearing Memorandum of Points and Authorities, at 1, ACLU v. Reno, 929 F. Supp. 824, 1996.

9. Jamie Le, "The Digital Divide: How the Online Behavior of Teens Is Getting Past Parents," McAfee.com, June 2012, http://www.mcafee.com/us/resources/misc/digital-divide-study.pdf.

10. Kaiser Family Foundation, "Generation RX.com: How Young People Use the Internet for Health Information," December 2001, http://kff.org/health-costs/report/generation-rx-com-how-young-people-use/.

11. This is a general statement, and there are always exceptions to it. See Proverbs 5:18–19; Matthew 5:28; Job 31:1.

12. "Why I Stopped Watching Porn," video clip, accessed August 26, 2015, YouTube, https://www.youtube.com/watch?v=gRJ_QfP2mhU.

13. Al Vernacchio, *For Goodness Sex: Changing the Way We Talk to Teens about Sexuality, Values, and Health* (New York: Harper Wave, 2014), 230. This is a good book from someone who works in the sex education field. His messages are inclusive and accepting, yet he also makes sure to emphasize that in many circumstances, someone's religious beliefs and values state what is acceptable and not acceptable. It's well balanced without graphic depictions if you are interested in reading a mainstream book on educating children and teens about sex.

14. "What is fMRI?" Center for Functional MRI, accessed August 26, 2015, http://fmri.ucsd.edu/Research/whatisfmri.html: "*Functional magnetic resonance imaging* (fMRI) is a technique for measuring and mapping brain activity that is noninvasive and safe. It is being used in many studies to better understand how the healthy brain works, and in a growing number of studies it is being applied to understand how that normal function is disrupted in disease."

15. M. E. Ehrlich, J. Sommer, E. Canas, and E. M. Unterwald, "Sexuality in Adolescence: The Digital Generation," *The Journal of Neuroscience* (2002): 22:9155–59.

16. Betsy Schiffman, "Turns Out Porn Isn't Recession-Proof," *Wired*, July 21, 2008, http://www.wired.com/2008/07/turns-out-por-1/.

17. If you haven't already, please read pages 155–57 to understand how the addiction process works.

18. D. Zillmann, "Influence of Unrestrained Access to Erotica on Adolescents' and Young Adults' Dispositions Toward Sexuality," *Journal of Adolescent Health* 27 (2000): 41–44.

19. Patrick Carnes, *Don't Call It Love: Recovery from Sexual Addiction* (New York: Bantam, 1991).

20. Jose Pagliery, "The Deep Web You Don't Know About," CNN Money, March 10, 2014, http://money.cnn.com/2014/03/10/technology/deep-web/index.html.

21. "Bitcoin Calculator," CoinDesk, accessed August 26, 2015, http://www.coindesk.com/calculator/.

22. *Juvenile Justice Bulletin* (Washington, DC: US Department of Justice, July 2010).

23. US Department of Justice, National Center for Missing and Exploited Children as reported in "Trafficked Teen Girls Describe Life in 'The Game,'" *All Things Considered*, December 6, 2010, http://www.npr.org/2010/12/06/131757019/youth-radio-trafficked-teen-girls-describe-life-in-the-game.

24. US Department of State, "Victims' Stories," *Trafficking in Persons Report 2011*, accessed September 24, 2015, http://www.state.gov/j/tip/rls/tiprpt/2011/164225.htm.

Chapter 5 Sexually Abused Children Rarely Speak Up

1. The National Child Traumatic Stress Network, *Child Sexual Abuse Fact Sheet*, April 2009, http://nctsn.org/nctsn_assets/pdfs/caring/ChildSexualAbuseFactSheet.pdf.

2. Stop It Now!, "Behaviors to Watch for When Adults Are with Children," Stop It Now!, accessed August 27, 2015, http://www.stopitnow.org/ohc-content/behaviors-to-watch-out-for-when-adults-are-with-children.

Resources for the Conversation

1. Howard Kopolowitz, "Whisper App Rape: Ronald Peterson III Arrested For Allegedly Raping 12-Year-Old Washington Girl He Met Through Secrets App," *International Business Times*, October 22, 2013, http://www.ibtimes.com/whisper-app-rape-ronald-peterson-iii-arrested-allegedly-raping-12-year-old-washington-girl-he-met.

Anne Marie Miller is the author of five books and has been featured in publications such as *Cosmopolitan*, *Relevant Magazine*, *Leadership Journal*, *Christianity Today*, *Neue*, *Reject Apathy*, *Youth Worker Journal*, *Outreach Magazine*, PurposeDriven.com, ChurchLeaders.com, *The United Methodist Reporter*, and BeliefNet.com. She speaks frequently at colleges, conventions, and churches in the United States and internationally. Anne Marie and her husband, Tim, live in Iowa. Learn more at www.annemariemiller.com.

FAITH · SEX · MENTAL HEALTH

Anne Marie Miller

5THINGSBOOK.COM

f Facebook.com/GirlNamedAnne

🐦 @GirlNamedAnne

📷 GirlNamedAnne

#5ThingsBook

Anne Marie Miller • 3500 Dodge Street Suite 205, Box 219 • Dubuque, IA 52003